1 AND 2 KINGS

FORTRESS COMMENTARY ON THE BIBLE

Fortress Commentary on the Bible: The Old Testament and Apocrypha
Fortress Commentary on the Bible: The New Testament
The Pentateuch: Fortress Commentary on the Bible Study Edition
The Prophets: Fortress Commentary on the Bible Study Edition
Wisdom, Worship, and Poetry: Fortress Commentary on the Bible Study Edition
The Historical Writings: Fortress Commentary on the Bible Study Edition
The Gospels and Acts: Fortress Commentary on the Bible Study Edition
The Letters and Legacy of Paul: Fortress Commentary on the Bible Study Edition
Hebrews, the General Epistles, and Revelation: Fortress Commentary on the Bible Study Edition
1 and 2 Kings: Fortress Commentary on the Bible
Isaiah: Fortress Commentary on the Bible
Mark: Fortress Commentary on the Bible
1 and 2 Corinthians: Fortress Commentary on the Bible

1 AND 2 KINGS

FORTRESS COMMENTARY ON THE BIBLE

GALE A. YEE

FORTRESS PRESS
Minneapolis

1 AND 2 KINGS
Fortress Commentary on the Bible

31 30 29 28 27 26 25 1 2 3 4 5 6 7 8 9

Library of Congress Cataloging-in-Publication Data

Names: Yee, Gale A., author
Title: 1 & 2 Kings : Fortress commentary on the Bible / Gale A. Yee.
Other titles: 1 and 2 Kings
Description: Minneapolis : Fortress Press, [2026]
Identifiers: LCCN 2025031604 (print) | LCCN 2025031605 (ebook) | ISBN 9798341900097 paperback | ISBN 9798341900103 ebook
Subjects: LCSH: Bible. Kings--Commentaries
Classification: LCC BS1335.53 .Y44 2006 (print) | LCC BS1335.53 (ebook)
LC record available at https://lccn.loc.gov/2025031604
LC ebook record available at https://lccn.loc.gov/2025031605

Cover design: Kris E. Miller
Cover image: compilation of stock textures from Getty Images

Print ISBN: 979-8-3419-0009-7
eBook ISBN: 979-8-3419-0010-3

CONTENTS

CONTRIBUTORS

Gale A. Yee
Nancy W. King Professor of Biblical Studies
Episcopal Divinity School

Volume Editors

Gale A. Yee
Nancy W. King Professor of Biblical Studies
Episcopal Divinity School

Hugh R. Page Jr.
Associate Professor of Theology and Africana Studies
Vice President, Associate Provost, and Dean of the First Year of Studies
University of Notre Dame

Matthew J. M. Coomber
Assistant Professor of Biblical Studies
St. Ambrose University

ABBREVIATIONS

General

DH	Deuteronomistic History
Dtr	Deuteronomist
LXX	The Septuagint

Books of the Bible (NT, OT, Apocrypha)

Old Testament/Hebrew Bible

Gen.	Genesis
Exod.	Exodus
Lev.	Leviticus
Num.	Numbers
Deut.	Deuteronomy
Josh.	Joshua
Judg.	Judges
Ruth	Ruth
1 Sam.	1 Samuel
2 Sam.	2 Samuel
1 Kgs.	1 Kings
2 Kgs.	2 Kings
1 Chron.	1 Chronicles
2 Chron.	2 Chronicles
Ezra	Ezra
Neh.	Nehemiah
Esther	Esther
Job	Job
Ps. (Pss.)	Psalms

Prov.	Proverbs
Eccles.	Ecclesiastes
Song.	Song of Songs
Isa.	Isaiah
Jer.	Jeremiah
Lam.	Lamentations
Ezek.	Ezekiel
Dan.	Daniel
Hosea	Hosea
Joel	Joel
Amos	Amos
Obad.	Obadiah
Jon.	Jonah
Mic.	Micah
Nah.	Nahum
Hab.	Habakkuk
Zeph.	Zephaniah
Hag.	Haggai
Zech.	Zechariah
Mal.	Malachi

Apocrypha

Tob.	Tobit
Jth.	Judith
Gk. Esther	Greek Additions to Esther
Sir.	Sirach (Ecclesiasticus)
Bar.	Baruch
Let. Jer.	Letter of Jeremiah
Add Dan.	Additions to Daniel
Pr. Azar.	Prayer of Azariah
Sg. Three.	Song of the Three Young Men (or Three Jews)
Sus.	Susanna
Bel	Bel and the Dragon
1 Macc.	1 Maccabees
2 Macc.	2 Maccabees
1 Esd.	1 Esdras
Pr. of Man.	Prayer of Manasseh
2 Esd.	2 Esdras
Wis.	Wisdom of Solomon

3 Macc.	3 Maccabees
4 Macc.	4 Maccabees

New Testament

Matt.	Matthew
Mark	Mark
Luke	Luke
John	John
Acts	Acts of the Apostles
Rom.	Romans
1 Cor.	1 Corinthians
2 Cor.	2 Corinthians
Gal.	Galatians
Eph.	Ephesians
Phil.	Philippians
Col.	Colossians
1 Thess.	1 Thessalonians
2 Thess.	2 Thessalonians
1 Tim.	1 Timothy
2 Tim.	2 Timothy
Titus	Titus
Philem.	Philemon
Heb.	Hebrews
James	James
1 Pet.	1 Peter
2 Pet.	2 Peter
1 John	1 John
2 John	2 John
3 John	3 John
Jude	Jude
Rev.	Revelation (Apocalypse)

Journals, Series, Reference Works

ABD	*Anchor Bible Dictionary*. Edited by David Noel Freedman. 6 vols. New York: Doubleday, 1992.
ANET	*Ancient Near Eastern Texts Relating to the Old Testament*.Edited by J. B. Pritchard. 3rd ed. Princeton: Princeton University Press, 1969.

BZAW	BeiheftezurZeitschriftfür die alttestamentlicheWissenschaft
CBQMS	Catholic Biblical Quarterly Monograph Series
ETL	*Ephemerides TheologicaeLovanienses*
IBC	Interpretation: A Bible Commentary for Teaching and Preaching
JAOS	*Journal of the American Oriental Society*
JBL	*Journal of Biblical Literature*
JSOT	*Journal for the Study of the Old Testament*
JSOTSup	Journal for the Study of the Old Testament Supplement Series
NovT	*NovumTestamentum*
PL	John Milton, *Paradise Lost*
VT	*VetusTestamentum*

Ancient Authors and Texts

Josephus

Ant.	*Jewish Antiquities*

Mishnah, Talmud, Targum

b. Meg.	*Babylonian Talmudic tractate Megillah*
b. Sanh.	*Babylonian Talmudic tractate Sanhedrin*
b. Yoma	*Babylonian Talmudic tractate Yoma*
Eccl. Rab.	*Ecclesiastes Rabbah*
Exod. Rab.	*Exodus Rabbah*
Gen. Rab.	*Genesis Rabbah*
Lam. Rab.	*Lamentations Rabbah*
Lev. R(ab).	*Leviticus Rabbah*

1 Kings

Introduction

LIKE THE BOOKS of Samuel, 1 and 2 Kings was originally one book in the Hebrew canon, continuing the story of the monarchy's decline that was readily apparent from 2 Samuel 9, which recounted the dysfunctional family relations in King David's household, onward. The book of Kings narrates the stories about David's son Solomon, the division into two kingdoms after Solomon's death, the events leading up to the conquest of the northern kingdom of Israel by the Assyrians, and finally to the destruction and exile of Judah by the Babylonians.

Composition

Critical examination of the book of Kings was important for theories about the composition of a major portion of the Old Testament (for a fuller discussion, see Römer). In 1943, the German scholar Martin Noth argued that the final form of the books of Deuteronomy, Joshua, Judges, 1–2 Samuel, and 1–2 Kings was due to a single individual working during the Babylonian exile in the sixth century BCE. Because these books shared similar theological themes and concepts with the book of Deuteronomy, Noth referred to these books collectively as the "Deuteronomistic History" (DH), and called its author/editor the "Deuteronomist" (Dtr). As an editor, Dtr conscientiously incorporated older documents and traditions for his work, such as the stories about the prophets Elijah and Elisha. Dtr even named some of his sources: "the Book of the Acts of Solomon" (1 Kgs. 11:41); "the Book of the Annals of the Kings of Judah" (1 Kgs. 14:29); and "the Book of the Annals of the Kings of Israel" (1 Kgs. 16:27). However, as an author, Dtr shaped these sources and older traditions to compose a particular narrative history of the two kingdoms that articulates his own theological intents and purposes.

American scholar Frank Moore Cross built on Noth's theory by positing a "double-redaction" of the DH. Instead of a single individual working during the exile, Cross noticed an earlier version of the DH that concluded in 2 Kings 22–23, describing the achievements of King Josiah in the seventh century BCE. This first edition of the DH ended with 2 Kgs. 23:25: "Before [Josiah] there was no king like him, who turned to the LORD with all his heart, with all his soul, and with all his might, according to all the law of Moses; nor did any like him arise after him." This Josianic edition underscored two themes. The first was YHWH's promises to David's dynasty in Judah, in spite of the fact that some of the Judean kings kept some of the "high places" of worship. The second was the "sin of Jeroboam," worship at the illegitimate sanctuaries of Dan and Bethel that infected practically every northern monarch and precipitated the ultimate fall of Israel. These two themes converged with the stories about Josiah, who destroyed the altar at Bethel and purged the nation of its idolatrous gods and practices. This seventh-century Josianic edition was then updated in a Deuteronomistic school to form a sixth-century exilic edition of the DH. Other scholars have even posited further editions during the Persian period (late sixth–fifth centuries BCE). The Deuteronomists responsible for these editions were probably high officials of the scribal class in Judah that shared a particular ideology and rhetorical style (Römer, 45–49).

Sense Units

This commentary divides 1 and 2 Kings into the following sense units:

1 Kgs. 1:1–2:46: Solomon's Succession to the Throne
1 Kgs. 3:1–28: Solomon the "Wise" Man?
1 Kgs. 4:1–11:42: Solomon's Bureaucratic Rule
1 Kgs. 12:1–16:34: The Divided Kingdom

1 Kgs. 17:1–22:53: The Ministries of the Prophets Elijah and Micaiah
2 Kgs. 1:1–8:29: The Ministry of the Prophet Elisha
2 Kgs. 9:1–12:21: The Rise of the House of Jehu and the Demise of the House of Omri
2 Kgs. 13:1–17:41: Events Leading to the Fall of Israel
2 Kgs. 18:1–20:21: The Reign of Hezekiah
2 Kgs. 21:1–23:30: The Reigns of Manasseh and Josiah
2 Kgs. 23:31–25:30: The Final Days of Judah and Its Kings

Theological Framework

Beginning in 1 Kings 15, after the narratives regarding Jeroboam I, Dtr provides a specific theological framework to introduce each of the ruling monarchs that will continue to the end of 2 Kings. The kings of Judah are presented according to the following pattern:

- The date the king took office, correlated with the rule of his rival in Israel (15:1—"In the eighteenth year of King Jeroboam son of Nebat, Abijam began to reign over Judah.")
- His length of reign (15:2a—"He reigned for three years in Jerusalem.")
- The name of the queen mother (15:2b—"His mother's name was Maacah daughter of Abishalom.")
- Dtr's judgment on his rule (15:3–5—"He committed all the sins that his father did before him . . .")
- Other deeds, if any (15:6—"The war begun between Rehoboam and Jeroboam continued all the days of his life.")
- Citation of sources (15:7—"The rest of the acts of Abijam, and all that he did, are they not written in the Book of the Annals of the Kings of Judah?")
- Burial (15:8a—"Abijam slept with his ancestors, and they buried him in the city of David.")
- Name of successor (15:8b—"Then his son Asa succeeded him.")

For the kings of Israel, Dtr follows a similar pattern, but adds the city in Israel where the king had his capital and omits the name of the queen mother: "In the third year of King Asa of Judah, Baasha son of Ahijah began to reign over all Israel at Tirzah; he reigned twenty-four years. He did what was evil in the sight of the Lord . . ." (1 Kgs. 15:33–34).

The most important section in this framework is Dtr's judgment on the king's rule. A certain king may have been a very capable leader, economically and politically. Or the king may have been caught up in the larger imperial politics of the ancient Near East that may have influenced his religious policies. The Dtr, however, is only concerned with how faithful he was to God's covenant. For him, "evil" kings were those who worshiped other gods or allowed their worship in the land; those who allowed shrines and sanctuaries to YHWH, such as the "high places" outside of Jerusalem; those who did not listen to God's prophets; those who participated in religious rituals that Dtr regarded as illicit. According to Dtr, the ultimate destruction of both Israel and Judah was due to their infidelity to YHWH alone by worshiping foreign gods from the moment the people crossed the Jordan and entered the land promised to their ancestors.

1 Kings 1:1–2:46

Solomon's Succession to the Throne

The Text in Its Ancient Context

First Kings 1–2 provides a literary bridge from the end of 2 Samuel to 1 Kings. First Kings begins forebodingly, with the detail that old King David could not get warm. Instead of piling on yet another blanket, his servants search the land for a young virgin who will join his harem to be his attendant and share his bed. One of the hallmarks of a king's royal status is the number of his wives, concubines, and sons, and David accumulated many as he gained power (see 2 Sam. 3:2–5; 5:13; 16:20–23). Scholars have remarked on the different ways David's private relationships with his women reflect issues in his public life (Berlin). Because David is unable to "know" Abishag sexually in spite of her beauty, she becomes a signifier of the impotence of his leadership at the end of his rule. The biblical author, as is typical, does not provide access to Abishag's thoughts about being taken from her home to service the king sexually.

Because of his deterioration and the fact that he has not named an heir, David's sons jockey to replace him. Solomon's rival is his half-brother Adonijah son of Haggith, who is not only next in line but good looking to boot. Adonijah presumptuously declares, "I will be king," and, like his older brother Absalom, who also had royal ambitions (2 Sam. 15:1–7), gathers a small band of chariots, horsemen, and fifty men to run before him. The declining David does not reproach him for his displays of royal privilege (1:5–6).

Adonijah has powerful people from the military and religious sectors of the kingdom supporting him: Joab, David's mighty general and son of David's sister Zeruiah, and Abiathar the priest. Solomon has his influential supporters as well: Zadok the priest, Nathan the prophet, Benaiah the leader of David's bodyguard, and his mother Bathsheba, the bathing beauty of 2 Samuel 11. Those supporting Adonijah go back to the time when David was king of Judah at Hebron. Those supporting Solomon only come on the scene when David moves his capital to Jerusalem. The parties thus represent the old guard versus the young "turks" in the dynamics of power (Ishida). The members of each party compete with each other for the same position in the realm: Adonijah and Solomon for the kingship; Haggith and Bathsheba as future queen mother; Joab and Benaiah as commander of the army; and Abiathar and Zadok as chief priest (1:7–8).

A sacrificial banquet, hosted by Adonijah, who invites all of David's sons and Judean officials but not Solomon or his supporters, becomes the catalyst for some harem politics to secure the throne for Solomon. Nathan the prophet exploits the jealousy and fears among royal wives to spur Bathsheba into action. He declares that the son of her rival Haggith has "become king" and gives her advice to save her own life and that of her son Solomon. He and Bathsheba cleverly maneuver an impotent, senile old king into proclaiming Solomon as his successor, and, with great fanfare, Solomon is anointed king at the spring of Gihon (1:9–40). When the news of this anointing reaches the banquet, Adonijah's guests abandon him and he himself flees to grasp the horns of the altar, its most sacred part. Solomon spares his life only on the condition that Adonijah "proves to be a worthy man" (1:41–53).

First Kings 2 begins with David on his deathbed giving his final instructions to Solomon. Exhibiting the hallmarks of Deuteronomistic redaction, David exhorts Solomon to adhere to God's covenantal demands as written in the torah/law of Moses in order to prosper in his rule (2:3). God's unconditional promise to David of an eternal dynasty (2 Samuel 7) now becomes conditioned upon the complete fidelity of his successors to God's commands (2:4). We will soon see that the rest of Kings narrates the failures of Israel and Judah to remain faithful to God, resulting ultimately in the destruction of the kingdom and the exile of the people at the end of the book. Solomon himself will initiate this falling-off by worshiping the gods of his many foreign wives (1 Kings 11). After his torah counsel, David instructs Solomon to assassinate Joab, David's right-hand man in military affairs, and Shimei, who had cursed him publicly (2:5–10). David then dies, ending a career riddled with murder by proxy (Halpern 2001).

In the next scene (2:13–46a), Adonijah, in either a shrewd or stupid move, asks Bathsheba to request from Solomon the hand of Abishag, David's last concubine, in marriage. Surprisingly or perhaps cleverly, Bathsheba agrees. The way Solomon behaves toward Bathsheba, rising up and bowing down in her presence and giving her a seat of honor, reveals the high position that Bathsheba achieves as mother of the king. This lends credibility to the notion that she understood very well the effect Adonijah's request would have on her son. Sexual relations with a woman from the former king's harem evoked strong responses in the male politics of gender (cf. 2 Sam. 3:7–8; 16:20–22). Solomon predictably interprets the request as a step to advance Adonijah's thwarted royal ambitions. He has Adonijah assassinated and then deals with Joab and Shimei according to his father's wishes. This unit concludes with the detail, "So the kingdom was established in the hand of Solomon" (2:46b).

The Text in the Interpretive Tradition

Much intriguing speculation exists on the voiceless minor character Abishag (Stahlberg). The Talmud records her saying to David, "Let us marry." When David replies, "Thou art forbidden to me," because he has attained his legal allotment of eighteen wives, she implicitly ridicules his impotence, at which point David shows that he still has what it takes in his old age and has sex with Bathsheba thirteen times (*Sanh.* 22a). Because she is from Shunem, Abishag is linked with the "black but/ and beautiful" Shulammite, Solomon's beloved (Song of Sol. 1:5; 6:13). Jerome allegorically personifies Abishag as wisdom herself, "so glowing as to warm the cold, yet so holy as not to arouse passion in him whom she warmed" (*Letter 52 to Nepotian* 2–3). She is the subject of a number of poems that reconstruct her feelings and experiences of being taken from her home to nurse and sleep with a decrepit king (Baumgarten; Curzon). The aging Earl of Hauberk in Aldous Huxley's *After Many a Summer* (1939) records in his diary, "I have tried King David's remedy against old age and found it wanting." In Stefan Heym's novel *The King David Report* (1972), Abishag is given a prominent, if not flattering role, as "stupidest woman in Israel," a sexually ripe concubine whose torrid affair with Adonijah leads to his downfall. In Joseph Heller's novel *God Knows* (1984), David's first love was and still is Bathsheba, who won't have anything to do with David, but still gives Abishag friendly advice about David's personal hygiene and eating habits.

The Text in Contemporary Discussion

Although royal males in their attempts to obtain the throne are the subject of 1 Kings 1–2, feminist scholars highlight the important roles that harem women play within these political dynamics. Abishag becomes a symbol of David's decline, and Adonijah's request for her hand in marriage leads to his murder. Bathsheba's collusion with Nathan successfully procures the throne for her son, and her sly request that Solomon approve Adonijah's bid for Abishag secures it.

In today's political arena, the wives of male politicians often exert tremendous influence on public policy, albeit informally and behind the scenes. Rosalind Carter and Nancy Reagan were First Ladies who had much influential sway on their presidential husbands. Only more recently have the wives of presidents, such as Hillary Rodham Clinton and Michelle Obama, assumed a more visible role.

1 Kings 3:1–28

Solomon the "Wise" Man?

The Text in Its Ancient Context

Now that his rivals have been eliminated, Solomon sets about consolidating his state and securing his rule over it. The first and last details describing Solomon's reign—his marriage to Pharaoh's daughter (3:1) and his love for his many foreign wives (11:1–10)—form a bracket around Solomon's story. Although his wisdom will be underscored throughout, the subtext of Solomon's narrative lays the blame for his decline on his unwise entanglements with foreign women, recurring Deuteronomistic specters thought to seduce Israel away from YHWH (Num. 25:1–3; Deut. 7:3–4; Josh. 23:11–13). His first foreign wife is the daughter of the Egyptian pharaoh, mentioned several times in this story (3:1; 7:8; 9:16, 24; 11:1–2). As a place of enslavement, genocide, and unrelenting oppression, Egypt occupies a significant negative site in the Israelite consciousness. And yet, Solomon seems to appropriate aspects of this empire in establishing his rule as his story unfolds: the large harem (beginning with the pharaoh's daughter), the procuring of "wisdom" (the province of the elite class, 4:30), the stratification of society into the haves and have-nots, the large building projects, the forced labor, the accumulation of wealth, and the brutal taxation.

Although Solomon "loved the LORD" (3:3), eventually building YHWH a great temple, he simultaneously "loved many foreign women" (11:1). Even though the adverse consequences of empire building will eventually lead to Solomon's deterioration, what the reader remembers is his love for foreign women and their gods, which seems to displace its real causes.

This tolerance for foreign religions is hinted in the report that Solomon often sacrificed at Gibeon, "the principal high place" (3:4). In Deuteronomistic theology, worship at the high places is usually forbidden, because Jerusalem is the central and normative locus of worship (1 Kgs. 12:31; 15:14; 22:43; 2 Kgs. 14:13, et passim). That Solomon is sacrificing in Gibeon when the ark resides in Jerusalem is rather unsettling. YHWH appears to him in a dream, saying: "Ask what I should give you" (3:5). Because he is only "a little child," faced with the task of governing "a great people," Solomon requests "an understanding mind" and the ability to "discern between good and evil" (3:9). Solomon's dream and the self-deprecating allusion to his youth parallel that of Tuthmoses IV of Egypt (*ANET* 449) and other propagandistic accounts that supply divine legitimation of a king's rule. Because Solomon asks for "understanding to discern what is right" (3:10) and does not ask for riches or honor, God will also give Solomon riches and honor all his life (3:13). Nevertheless, this promise to Solomon of wisdom, riches, and honor is conditional. Solomon must walk in the ways of YHWH, keeping God's statutes and commandments (3:14), a condition that Solomon will not always keep, as we shall see. The narrative ends with Solomon waking up from his dream, returning to Jerusalem to stand before the ark of the covenant. He then offers sacrifices and a feast at the only legitimate place of worship, according to the Deuteronomist (3:15).

Although it originally may have been an independent folktale about the judgment of an unknown ruler, the familiar account of the two prostitutes before Solomon now provides an illustration of Solomon's newly acquired wisdom (3:16–28). Various reasons why the story has two *prostitutes* before the king have been proposed: perhaps the designation explains why these women live together with infants but no husbands; perhaps to highlight that all levels of social strata were able to find justice before the king; perhaps to foreground Solomon's dilemma in deciding between two women, who were considered disreputable and deceptive by nature because of their occupation.

The contours of the case are filtered through the eyes of the plaintiff. According to the plaintiff, the defendant gave birth to a son three days after the birth of her own. During the night when no one else was in the house, the defendant's son dies because "she lay on him" (3:19). While the plaintiff slept, the defendant allegedly took the plaintiff's son and replaced him with her own dead son at the plaintiff's breast. When the plaintiff awoke to nurse, she discovered that her son was dead, but in a closer look knew that the infant was not her son. The defendant refutes her accuser by declaring, "No, the living son is mine and the dead son is yours," arguing back and forth before the king (3: 20–22). The king resolves the conflict by commanding a sword be brought and slicing the infant in two. The true mother is revealed when, moved with compassion, she pleads to the king to not kill her son, but give him to the other woman. The other woman declares: "It shall be neither mine nor yours; divide it" (3:24–26). The Hebrew text is ambiguous regarding the true mother. English versions, for example, the NRSV and NIB, have the king respond, "Give *the first woman* the living boy," even though the Hebrew only says, "Give her the living boy" (3:27), without clearly designating either the plaintiff or the defendant. Biblical scholars have argued for one or the other as the true mother (Garsiel 1993; Wolde).

Although this story ostensibly reveals Solomon's wisdom after God grants him this gift, the process leading toward his judgment would not pass muster in present-day courtrooms. Solomon simply accepts the testimony of the plaintiff without question and does not ask for the defendant's version of the case. He does not probe more deeply how the plaintiff knew that the defendant switched babies in the middle of the night if she was indeed asleep. Why did she not wake up when the dead baby was put at her breast (3:20)? Solomon does not investigate the crime scene for any clues. Instead, he rather recklessly endangers the life of an infant to provoke a reaction from the true mother.

Scholars have pointed out intertextual contrasts between 1 Kings 3 and 2 Kgs. 6:24–31, which also involves two mothers wrangling before the king over one living son. One of these mothers demonstrates compassion for her son; the other, a lack. However, their case is much more gruesome than the one judged by Solomon. During a siege that has been starving the population, the plaintiff had made a pact with the defendant to cook and eat her son that day, and the defendant's son the next day. However, after the plaintiff's son was consumed, the defendant reneged on her side of the bargain and hid her son. The king, seeing no way to resolve this dispute, tears his clothes and irrationally seeks vengeance on the prophet Elisha. Second Kings 6 seems to provide a negative counterpart to the all-wise Solomon, a negativity that is already imbedded in 1 Kings 3 (Lasine; Pyper).

The Text in the Interpretive Tradition

The story of Solomon's judgment over the prostitutes is perhaps the most well-known, interpreted, and even parodied of his narrative (Ipsen, 134–35). Ephrem the Syrian and Augustine interpreted the story as an allegory in which the two women represent the church and the synagogue, in which the Jews symbolized by the false mother kills her son Christ. Augustine also saw Jewish Christians who tried to enforce the law onto gentiles like the false mother (Conti, 15–21).

Because the text does not explicitly point out which woman is the true mother, the interpretive tradition had different ways to resolve the ambiguity. For example, Rabbi Joseph Kara (1065–1135 CE) thought one could distinguish between a day-old child and one who was three days old on the basis of the birth blood of each. Radbaz (1480–1574 CE) conjectured that Solomon noted the facial similarity between the living child and that of the plaintiff and between the dead infant and that of the defendant (Garsiel, 232–34).

In chapter 14 of Mark Twain's *Huckleberry Finn*, Jim provides a negative reading of this story, based on his experiences as an African American slave, to contradict Huck's understanding of Solomon as the "wisest man." Jim uses a dollar bill to substitute for the child desired by both women. A wise person would go around the neighborhood to find out to which of the two women the money belongs, and then hand it over to the right one. But Solomon would "whack de bill in *two*" and give the pieces to the two parties. Jim declares, "what's de use erdat half a bill?—can't buy noth'nwid it. En what use is a half a chile? I wouldn' give a dern for a million un um." Because Solomon had this large harem, he must have had " 'bout five million chillen-runnin' roun' de house." He does not value children as a man who only had one or two children. But Solomon, "*He* as soon chop a chile in two as a cat. Dey's plenty mo'. A chileer two, mo' er less, warn't no consekens to Sollermun, dad fatch him!" In the world of slavery, slaves are commodities that are bought and sold. Their intrinsic humanity to the slaveholder is of "no consekens." Jim thus comes off as a wiser man than Solomon in this chapter.

The Text in Contemporary Discussion

Of the Solomon traditions, the common lectionaries only contain selections of his dream at Gibeon (3:5–15) and of his prayer at the temple's dedication (8:22–30, 41–43). These readings highlight Solomon's wisdom and piety, while omitting his ruthless elimination of his rivals (1 Kings 2) and his adoption of the oppressive trappings of empire. For the people in the pews, they thus present a one-sided picture of Solomon that supports the idealized traditional reputation as a wise and discerning leader, a reputation that should be counterbalanced with a more critical assessment of his rule.

One of the bitterest aspects of divorce proceedings is over the custody of children. These proceedings often take months, even years, of expensive litigation and emotional turmoil. Although dividing the family property down the middle can be a fair distribution between divorcing partners, "splitting the baby" according to Solomonic justice cannot be an option when it comes to their children. Determining the best interests of the child in our day and age takes much more wisdom than that demonstrated by Solomon in this text.

Feminist scholarship has highlighted the fact that the only narrated example of Solomon's wisdom was on behalf of prostitutes. Within the economics of the texts, one of the most vulnerable members of society, widows who have no male family members to support them may have to resort to prostitution in order to survive. When one focuses on the perspective of the women as prostitutes, one considers the systemic economic circumstances that force women into prostitution, in ancient times and modern, and what kind of justice they can appeal to when their rights are violated (Bird, 197;Ipsen, 134).

1 Kings 4:1–11:42

Solomon's Bureaucratic Rule

The Text in Its Ancient Context

The different editorial and ideological layers in these chapters make it is difficult to determine their historical reliability about Solomon and his presumed tenth-century rule. Their narratives have analogues to eighth- and seventh-century-BCE Assyrian inscriptions, persuading scholars to regard them as later retrojections to create a magnificent past for Israel (see also Moore and Kelle, 244–57; Römer, 99). Although Solomon is depicted "in all his glory" (see Matt. 6:29 // Luke 12:27), there is a dark undercurrent revealing Solomon as just another dictatorial and oppressive king like those in other ancient Near Eastern empires. In order to secure his rule, Solomon reorganized his kingdom into twelve administrative districts that cut across tribal lines, staffing them with Judeans who had family or close ties with the Davidic dynasty (4:7–19). Through this redistricting, Solomon was able to constrain and exploit the powerful northern tribes through heavy tax burdens, from which his own tribe of Judah was exempt. First Kings 4:22–28 describes the exorbitant monthly demands from each of these districts, especially for luxury foods, such as meat, that go well beyond subsistence.

Solomon embarked on a number of expensive building projects to trumpet his successes and wealth, but these were realized at a heavy cost (1 Kings 5–7). He had to conscript thousands of his own people and foreigners into corvée labor groups to work on these buildings (4:6; 5:13–18; 9:20–21), taking them away from agricultural production, which was the major source of Israel's economy. The indigenous trees in Israel were not suitable for the great building projects that Solomon desired. In order to purchase and import the celebrated cedars of Lebanon, Solomon had to pay the foreign king Hyram of Tyre an enormous fee in wheat and fine oil (5:11), adding more to the people's tax burden.

The major and most famous building project was the Jerusalem temple (1 Kings 5–8). The three-part floor plan of the temple was similar to Canaanite temples that have been excavated from the same period. This is not surprising since Canaanite craftsmen were involved in the construction (see 7:13). The temple consisted of a vestibule, a nave, and an inner sanctuary, often referred to as the holy of holies (6:2–10). The construction reflected the stratification of the society. The three divisions marked the intensifying degrees of exclusivity, the vestibule having more public access; the nave, more limited; and the holy of holies, forbidden except to the most senior priests and only on special occasions. The rich latticework and carvings, the costly stones, the great bronze pillars and basins, the numerous vessels and accoutrements of gold and silver, and so forth (1 Kings 7) all have a flip side. This great extravagance for the few came at the cost borne by most of the population.

First Kings 6:1 notes that Solomon began this construction "in the four hundred eightieth year after the Israelites came out of the land of Egypt." Long after Israel was freed from Egyptian slavery, Israel ironically had to endure forced servitude and exploitation again under its own king. The building and its furnishings are described in all their opulence, but in the midst of these details of conspicuous consumption is an important condition in both the temple's construction and inauguration accounts: If Solomon obeys all of God's commandments, God will keep the promise made to David and dwell with Israel and not forsake them (6:11–13; cf. 8:56–61). Here the royal ideology of the monarchy that highlights God's promises to the Davidic dynasty stands in tension with the Mosaic covenantal demands that the people, including Israel's king, remain obedient to God's torah (Brueggemann, 88–89). We will soon see that Solomon was not successful in following God's commandments.

The section 1 Kgs. 9:10–11:42 narrates Solomon's downhill slide in his questionable dealings with foreign kings and foreign women, the slave labor of foreign peoples, his staggering greed, and his eventual idolatry. This decline is particularly evident when one compares 10:14–11:8 with Deut. 17:16–17, which stipulates that the king

- must not acquire horses for himself;
- must not return to Egypt in order to acquire more horses;
- must not acquire many wives for himself, or "else his heart will turn away";
- must also not amass silver and gold for himself in great quantity.

Solomon, however, commits all of these infractions in chapters 10–11, depicting a king who shaped his regime into the likeness of Egypt, who had oppressed their ancestors, sending his people back to Egypt to stockpile wealth and horses and adding women to his already substantial harem (Sweeney 2007, 146–47).

Solomon's rule, which began propitiously when Solomon "*loved* the Lord" (3:3), now comes to a shameful close because he "*loved* many foreign women," who turned his heart away from God to worship their own alien deities (11:1–8). Although a hint of disapproval exists, the Deuteronomist presents the negative economic aspects of Solomon's rule—the forced labor, his extreme taxation, his ostentatious materialism—rather neutrally, as opposed to the explicit censure of the king's economic exploitation found in 1 Sam. 8:10–18 and Dtr's advocacy for the most helpless in society (see Deut. 10:18; 24:17–22; 27:19). What comes under his unequivocal condemnation is Solomon's love of many foreign women, who persuade him to sacrifice to their gods.

The reader is left with the lasting impression that Solomon's downfall was due to his sexual relationships with women and not to his material self-indulgence and economic oppression (Jobling, 61–64). Because of these marriages, God raises up three major adversaries against Solomon (Hadad, Rezon, and Jeroboam), whose rebellions sow the seeds for the division of the kingdom after Solomon's death (11:14–43). The most significant of these adversaries is Jeroboam, who was in command of Solomon's forced labor in the tribe of Joseph (11:28). After receiving a prophecy from the prophet Ahijah that God will "tear the kingdom from the hand of Solomon" and give to Jeroboam the "ten tribes" (11:31), Jeroboam flees to Egypt, only to return after Solomon's death to become the first king of the northern kingdom (12:20).

The Solomon narrative concludes with the Deuteronomistic citation of its source (the Book of the Acts of Solomon), Solomon's length of rule in Jerusalem, his death, and his succession by his son Rehoboam (11:41–21).

The Text in the Interpretive Tradition

The parallel account of Solomon in 2 Chronicles 1–9 omits the negative stories of Solomon's idolatry and revolts in 1 Kings 11 and foregrounds the temple in its exposition.

A number of early Christian allegorical interpretations of Solomon's kingdom and temple exist (Conti, 24–64). For example, according to Ephrem the Syrian (c. 306–73 CE), the twelve officials who administered Solomon's kingdom (1 Kgs. 4:7) foreshadowed the twelve apostles of Jesus. The Venerable Bede (c. 672–735 CE) believed that the three floors of the temple (1 Kgs. 6:6) reflected a hierarchical ordering of the lifestyles of the faithful: married people, those who practice continence, and virgins, "levels distinguished according to the loftiness of their profession but all belonging to the house of the Lord" (Conti 2008, 31).

Over the centuries, Jewish and Muslim traditions have presented the story of Solomon and Sheba (1 Kgs. 10:1–13) as a contest of body and mind between an independent and boundary-crossing woman and a man who is eager to keep her subservient. By the Middle Ages, the main focus of the queen's visit had shifted from international to sexual politics, so that in postbiblical and Islamic versions, the queen's sparring match with Solomon was depicted as a threatening attempt to subvert the traditional roles of gender. In the same vein, an Ethiopian legend in the *KebraNegast* ("Glory of the Kings") records Solomon cleverly seducing the queen after she had made him swear that he not take her by force. They beget Menelik I, the first emperor of Ethiopia (Lassner 1993).

The Text in Contemporary Discussion

The Solomon narratives reveal that the steep income disparity between the haves and the have-nots that we see so blatantly in our own day is not a new phenomenon. Solomon heavily taxed his rural population for both material and human resources in order to support the luxurious lifestyles of his court and build his grandiose monuments. Each month, the court received from one of the provinces not only the choicest grains and flocks but also exotic animals like deer, gazelles, roebucks, and fatted fowl (4:22–24). Similarly, in our day, meat is usually found only on tables in the so-called first world and especially in the United States. Our excessive consumption of meat is having disastrous effects on the environment globally. Moreover, Solomon's forced labor gangs have some analogues to the trade in human trafficking today. Although the former is state-run, while the latter is illicit, both involve coercion and much human suffering.

These narratives are also cautionary tales for us today. They raise serious questions about the abuse of power by a nation's leadership. Solomon's disproportionate wealth and exploitation of the people to obtain it would have enormous consequences. Resistance and protests plagued the last days of his rule. Nowadays, we have food riots over grain and water shortages as a result of the diversion of good farmland to feed cattle, not people. History has already shown us that indifference of the wealthier classes to the poverty and destitution of the people often results in armed conflict. With Solomon, as we will see, this indifference resulted in the division of his kingdom. These texts obligate us to attend to the most vulnerable in our midst so that our global world does not fracture any more than it already has.

1 Kings 12:1–16:34

The Divided Kingdom

The Text in Its Ancient Context

Ahijah's prophecy in 11:31–40, that God will wrench the kingdom from Solomon and give to Jeroboam "the ten tribes," becomes fulfilled in this unit. After his father's death, Rehoboam goes up to be crowned in the important northern city of Shechem, perhaps as a positive gesture toward the northern tribes, or as a presumptuous declaration of his sovereignty over them (Seow, 100). Having heard that Solomon has died, Jeroboam, his rebellious corvee overseer, returns from Egypt where he had fled from Solomon's wrath (11:40). Along with the tribes, he urges the new king to lighten the hard service and heavy yoke that Solomon had imposed on them. Recall the daily extravagant provisions that the northern tribes had to supply the Jerusalem court (4:22–28) and the corvée labor that built Solomon's building projects (5:13–18). Rehoboam first consults his father's seasoned advisors, who recommend that he "lighten the yoke" appointed by his father. However, rejecting their advice, he turns to a group of courtiers he grew up with, disparagingly described as "boys" to underscore their contrast with the elders. These middle-aged associates—Rehoboam was evidently forty-one years old when he ascended the throne (14:21)—encourage a reply that hints at Rehoboam's or perhaps their own "daddy issues": "My little 'thingie' [Sweeney 2007, 163] is thicker than my father's loins!" (12:10). Given the seemingly huge size of Solomon's own harem (11:3), this would have been an extravagant claim by his arrogant offspring. Rehoboam then declares that rather than lightening the heavy yoke, he will intensify the burdens that his father had laid upon the people (12:14). Predictably, the northern tribes reject Rehoboam as king and return back to their homes. Rehoboam foolishly tries to regain control by dispatching Adoram, his official in charge of corvée labor, to the northern tribes, who promptly stone Adoram to death. Their next victim possibly would have been Rehoboam had he not hastily jumped into his chariot and fled back to Jerusalem (12:16–18).

As the newly crowned king of Israel (12:20), Jeroboam is confronted first with a political problem with religious implications. The Jerusalem temple and its cult continue to be a significant focus of the people's worship, because it houses the ark of the covenant. The northern tribes venerate the ark because it resided in several of their sanctuaries before it was brought to Jerusalem (Judg. 20:26–27; 1 Sam. 3:3; 6:21–7:1). Even though Ahijah prophesied that if Jeroboam follows God's statutes and commandments his dynasty will endure (11:38), Jeroboam still fears that allowing pilgrimages to Jerusalem will turn the people's allegiance back to Rehoboam. To prevent the cross-border excursions, he establishes two shrines at Dan and Bethel, polar ends of his kingdom, installing two calves of gold, of which he declares, "Here are your gods, O Israel, who brought you up out of the land of Egypt" (12:26–33). While the calves themselves are not idols, but simply the beasts of burden that carry the invisible God, for the Josianic Deuteronomist they become reified as "the sin of Jeroboam" throughout his history (see 1 Kgs. 13:34; 14:16; 2 Kgs. 3:3; 10:29; 13:2, et passim). From his southern perspective, the only legitimate place of worship is the temple in Jerusalem. In the dangerous memory of Israel, the calves also conjure up the image of the idolatrous golden calf that Aaron made for the Israelites in the wilderness, underscoring the illegitimacy of Jeroboam's cult (Exodus 32; see Knoppers, 92).

In the next episode, the Deuteronomist continues to portray the competitors of the Jerusalem cult as illicit. While Jeroboam is offering incense at Bethel, a man of God from Judah directs a prophecy at the altar, proclaiming that Josiah, a descendant from the Davidic dynasty several hundred years later, will sacrifice on this altar the priests of the high places established by Jeroboam (13:2–3; cf. 12:31–32). Later in the

DH, Josiah will eventually tear down this altar with its gruesome ashes and purge the land of its idolatrous cult (2 Kings 23).

Jeroboam's story ends tragically. When his son Abijah falls ill, Jeroboam tells his unnamed wife to disguise herself, go to Shiloh, and consult with Ahijah, the same prophet who had declared that Jeroboam would rule an enduring house like David's (11:38). However, because Jeroboam made for himself "other gods and cast images," provoking God to anger, Ahijah now proclaims that God will put an end of his dynasty (14:7–11). Ahijah then orders the wife back home, prophesying her son's death, which comes to pass when she crosses the threshold of her house. The seeming passivity of the wife prompts feminists to speculate whether the wife was a victim of domestic violence (Branch, 83–107).

From this point on, the Deuteronomist provides a particular theological frame for the rival kings of Israel and Judah (see the introduction). The most important part of his framework is his religious judgment on the rule, whether he obeyed God's law and banished idols, high places, and so on from the land or let them flourish. A particular king may have been an important political leader and good ruler, but is condemned by the Dtr for religious reasons. For example, given the propensity in Israel for regicide (assassination of kings; see 1 Kgs. 15:27; 16:9–10, 15–16), it is significant that the kings who had the longest reigns in Israel are censured by the Dtr: Jeroboam I (twenty-two years), Basha (twenty-four years), Ahab (twenty-two years), and Jeroboam II (forty-one years).

The Text in the Interpretive Tradition

A version of the LXX contains an alternative account that portrays Jeroboam more negatively (Sweeney 2007, 165–67). Although 12:26 describes his mother Zeruah as a widow (11:26), in this version she is a prostitute named Sarira. The unidentified wife of Jeroboam also receives a name. When Jeroboam flees to Egypt from Solomon's anger, the pharaoh Sausakim (MT Shishak, 12:40) gives him his sister-in-law,

Ano, as wife, who bears him a son, Abijah. The version then recounts Jeroboam's gathering the Israelite tribes at Shechem and building fortifications there. At this point, Abijah becomes sick and Jeroboam directs Ano to seek God's counsel. Abijah dies, according to the prophecy Ahijah gives to Ano (see 14:12–13, 17–18). The LXX expansion highlights Rehoboam as an immature teenager and insinuates Jeroboam's role in instigating the revolt by placing him in Israel before the North's rebellion. Jeroboam's marriage into Shishak's royal family reinforces Jeroboam's culpability even more when Shishak later invades Judah after the division (14:25–28).

The Old Testament figure of Ahab was one of the biblical prototypes for Captain Ahab in Herman Melville's *Moby-Dick*. Because Jeroboam is Ahab's predecessor and the prophetic condemnation of the kings of Israel because of his "sin" (see 15:25) will determine the fate of Ahab, his story finds a particular analogue in Melville's tome. The ship *Jeroboam* in *Moby-Dick* becomes the forerunner of Captain Ahab's *Pequod*, and two members of its crew correspond to members of Jeroboam's household: the death of the shipmate Macey parallels Jeroboam's stricken son Abijah, and Gabriel parallels the prophet Ahijah (Bartel, 44–46).

The Text in Contemporary Discussion

Lord Acton remarked in a letter to Bishop Mandell Creighton in 1887: "Power tends to corrupt, and absolute power corrupts absolutely. Great men are almost always bad men." Rehoboam's folly in not heeding the wisdom of his older advisors presents a cautionary tale about leadership and the abuse of power. In response to the people's request to ease up on the heavy burdens his father had laid on them, Rehoboam arrogantly responds: "Whereas my father laid on you a heavy yoke, I will add to your yoke. My father disciplined you with whips, but I will discipline you with scorpions" (12:11). History throughout reveals that tyrannical rulers and oppressive systems of power will face resistance when the subjugated will not take it anymore: from the slave rebellions against

Rome, to the civil rights marches against racism of the last century, to the recent Occupy movement against corporate greed. The text raises questions about what it means to be a leader. Is it true that power corrupts and absolute power corrupts absolutely? How do we prevent or resist the corruption of power without becoming corrupt ourselves?

1 Kings 17:1–22:53

The Ministries of the Prophets Elijah and Micaiah

The Text in Its Ancient Context

These chapters highlight the ministries of the prophets Elijah (chs. 17–19, 21) and Micaiah (ch. 22) in their clashes with King Ahab of Israel (c. 873–852 BCE) of the powerful royal dynasty of Omri. According to 16:29–34, Ahab not only walked in the sins of Jeroboam but also angered God even more by marrying a foreign woman, Jezebel, daughter of the king of the Sidonians, and worshiping her gods Baal and Asherah. Recall that Solomon's marriages to foreign women and his apostasy led to his own deterioration (1 Kings 11). Also important in understanding these chapters is that both the kings of Israel and Judah continued Solomon's exploitative economic policy of extracting the surpluses from their agrarian subjects to support their building projects, wars, and extravagant lifestyles. This one-sided systemic extraction resulted in the impoverishment of the nation's peasant base.

In 17:1, Elijah appears out of nowhere to proclaim a drought in God's name that will afflict Israel. This declaration is a direct polemic against the worship of the Baal, the Canaanite god responsible for rain and fertility in the land. Although the veneration of Canaanite deities is expressly condemned in the Hebrew Bible, this represents only a part, though an important one, of the rich pluralism in Israelite belief and practice. The worship of Baal and even the goddess Asherah was accepted or at least tolerated in the early stages of Israel's religious development (Dever; M. S. Smith 2002). However, not only does 1 Kgs.

17–22 reflect the developing "Yahweh-alone" theology that belittled these deities (Lang, 13–56; M. Smith 1971, 34–37), but their worship is linked to a royal system of exploitation, in which the majority of the population suffered under the oppression of a small group of ruling elites (Brueggemann 2000, 202–3). Misery from the three-year drought particularly afflicted the marginalized classes of society, as is evident in Elijah's encounter with the starving widow and her malnourished son in Jezebel's own Phoenician hometown of Sidon (17:8–34). Meanwhile, Jezebel murders God's own prophets (18:4, 13), but hosts banquets for the 450 prophets of Baal and the 400 prophets of Asherah, while the rest of the nation starves (18:19). Ahab too seems more concerned about grass for his horses and mules than food for his own people (18:5). According to the Kurkh Monolith, Ahab possessed enough horses to pull two thousand chariots in a campaign against the Assyrian king Shalmaneser III (Grabbe 2007, 131, 142–43). However, Obadiah's protection of God's prophets from Jezebel's persecution reveals that even some high-level members of the royal court resisted the oppressive policies (18:3, 13).

The confrontation on Mount Carmel between YHWH and Baal is about who can end the drought and bring rain to the land. It is also about the religio-political systems that undergird their worship (18:20–46). This narrative dramatically pits the 450 prophets of Baal against God's lone prophet, Elijah. Two altars for two bulls are prepared. The challenge is which god will answer by fire to consume his sacrificial altar. The Baal prophets go first, calling out to their god from morning till noon with no answer. Elijah taunts their efforts, and they set about gashing themselves, intensifying their raving until past midday with no response. Then, in some spectacularly theatrical moves, Elijah builds an altar with twelve stones symbolizing the twelve tribes of Israel and digs a large trench around it. He dismembers his bull and places the pieces on the wood of the altar. He commands four jars of waters be splashed on the altar three times. He prays one little prayer and immediately God answers with fire, consuming the whole altar and even the water in the trench. Elijah has all the prophets of Baal assassinated, and then tells

Ahab to eat and drink, "for there is a sound of rushing rain" (18:41), proving that YHWH, not Baal, makes the life-giving waters flow.

The next clash between Elijah and Ahab, which occurs in 1 Kings 21, foregrounds the ruling elite's abuse of power over land ownership. Ahab wants a vineyard in Jezreel belonging to a man named Naboth, who refuses Ahab's offer of either a better vineyard or a reasonable price, because he regards the land as an inheritance that should not be bought or sold outside of the family to which it belonged (see Num. 27:1–11; Deut. 25:5–10; Jer. 32:6–12). Knowing Mosaic custom, Ahab reacts by pouting and refusing to eat, whereupon Jezebel admonishes him, saying basically, "Aren't you the one who rules Israel?" (21:1–7). Jezebel regards land as a tradable commodity to which the monarch has a privileged claim (Brueggemann 2000, 257–65). She instigates an illegitimate seizure of his land and engineers his death (21:8–16). God then orders Elijah to meet Ahab and prophesy his death sentence because of his wife's deeds: "Thus says the Lord: In the place where dogs licked up the blood of Naboth, dogs will also lick up your blood" (21:19). Jezebel also does not escape censure: "The dogs shall eat Jezebel within the bounds of Jezreel" (21:23).

Elijah seemingly disappears in 1 Kings 20 and 22, but Ahab does not. These chapters deal with Ahab's wars with the Arameans (present-day Syria; for the historical problems dealing with chs. 20 and 22, see Sweeney 2007, 237–58). Although a number of anonymous prophets interact with Ahab in 20:13–15, 22, 28, 35–42, the major prophet confronting Ahab in 1 Kings 22 has a name: Micaiah. Three years have passed since Ahab last fought, but then later made a peace treaty with, the king of Aram (22:1; see 1 Kings 20). Because of this ill-advised treaty, an unnamed prophet condemns Ahab to death (20:42), a sentence that will be fulfilled in 1 Kings 22. Ahab makes an alliance with Jehoshaphat, the king of Judah (c. 870–846 BCE), to recapture Ramoth-Gilead, a strategically important city near the border between Israel and Aram. Jehoshaphat first wants to consult the "word of YHWH" before entering into combat (22:5). Because war involved the participation of YHWH the Divine Warrior, it was a holy affair. Kings thus did not commence battle without consulting the prophets, who informed them about the divine will.

Ahab thus assembles four hundred court prophets and asks if he should go into battle. Though they guarantee his victory, Jehoshaphat still wants another prophetic opinion. Ahab replies that there is another prophet, Micaiah, who can be consulted, "but I hate him, for he never prophesies anything favorable about me, but only disaster" (22:8). Nevertheless, at Jehoshaphat's prompting, Ahab sends for Micaiah, while the court prophets continue to affirm Ahab's victory over the Arameans (22:9–12).

When Ahab asks Micaiah whether the army shall proceed against Ramoth-Gilead, Micaiah prophesies victory. Suspicious of this response in light of past experience, Ahab demands Micaiah to tell "the truth in the name of YHWH" (22:15–16). Micaiah responds with two visions, the first of Israel scattered like sheep without a shepherd, and the second of God in his heavenly court, who asks for a volunteer to be a lying spirit in the mouths of Ahab's prophets. The gist of these visions is that the Lord has decreed disaster for Ahab (22:17–23). Ahab indeed dies ignobly by the end of the chapter (22:29–36). His bloody chariot is washed by the pool of Samaria. Dogs lick up his blood, fulfilling Elijah's prophecy (21:19), and to add insult to injury, prostitutes also wash themselves in it (22:37–38). First Kings concludes with the ascension of his son Ahaziah to the throne, who not only continues the "sin of Jeroboam" but also walks in the way of his father and mother, citing both Ahab and Jezebel in their idolatrous worship of Baal (22:51–53).

The Text in the Interpretive Tradition

According to the final verses of the book of Malachi, God will send Elijah before "the great and terrible day of the Lord" (4:5). Elijah thus will be seen as the harbinger of the Messiah in Jewish tradition. At Passover celebrations, a cup is usually left out for the arrival of Elijah.

Elijah is included in Sirach's "praises of famous men" (Sir. 48:1–12). In the Christian ordering of the books of the Hebrew Bible, the book of Malachi is placed last in the canon, immediately before the Gospels, so that Elijah appears to herald the coming of Jesus. The Gospels describe John the Baptist, the forerunner of Jesus, in the manner of Elijah, a "hairy man, with a leather belt around his waist (2 Kgs. 1:8; cf. Matt. 3:4; 11:14; 17:10–13; Luke 1:16–17). Elijah also appears at Jesus' transfiguration on the mountain along with Moses (Matt. 17:1–13; Mark 9:2–13; Luke 9:28–36). Elijah is one of the prophets referred to in the Quran as a precursor of Muhammad. Martin Luther compared Elijah to the Reformers, and the prophets of Baal to the Roman Catholic Church. In some Jewish legends, the son of the widow of Zarephath, whom Elijah healed (17:17–24), will later become the prophet Jonah.

Ahab's wife, Jezebel, was most likely a very powerful woman in her time, part of the ruling class of an agrarian society, wielding considerable authority in her position as queen. However, she has been demonized even in the early developments of the tradition. The *zebul* of her original name, "Prince, nobility," was distorted into *zebel*, "dung" (Dutcher-Walls 2004; Yee, 848). In the New Testament, the book of Revelation depicts a strong woman "who calls herself a prophet" as a Jezebel, seducing her flock into fornication and idolatry (Rev. 2:19–23). Modern-day dictionaries have also nominalized her name to describe a shameless, scheming woman. This characterization can be found in numerous depictions of Jezebel and women like her in theological treatises, sermons, novels, poetry, and theater (Gaines; Snyder). She is perhaps most memorably embodied in the actress Bette Davis as a spoiled, conniving southern belle in the motion picture *Jezebel* (Warner Bros., 1938). (For a semifictional account of Jezebel by a biblical scholar that tries to rehabilitate her notoriety, see Beach 2005.)

The Text in Contemporary Discussion

Prophets emerged in ancient Israel during the time of the monarchy to announce God's judgments regarding a particular king's wars, foreign agreements, religious allegiances, and domestic economic and political policies. They condemned a king's abuses of power. They were also described as performing miracles, healing the sick, and making fire come down from the sky.

The question these texts raise for us now is whether such prophets exist in our own time. The stereotype of a prophet is that of a fortune-teller, one who sees and predicts the future. A prophet should be regarded instead as one who sees and analyzes the *present*, one who reads the signs of the times and declares the disastrous future results if things do not change. Such a person must be knowledgeable of contemporary affairs and skilled in some sort of social analysis to critique any injustice or exploitation. Individuals, such as social activists, public policy makers, ecologists, artists, poets, and musicians can all be prophetic in their own way.

Ahab and Jezebel's seizure of Naboth's land has disturbing parallels throughout history in which colonizers from Europe seized lands in Asia, Latin America, and Africa, robbing their indigenous peoples of their rich resources. This colonization continues in our own global economy today, where big corporations exploit the so-called third world of its resources and cheap labor for money and profit. Land and its inhabitants become commodities that can be bought and sold. Where are the prophets today who will hold these corporations accountable?

Popular culture usually lists Jezebel as one of the "bad girls of the Bible." Such stereotyping affects all women who are powerful, competent, independent, and forceful. Qualities that are usually admired in men are depicted as "bossy, pushy, aggressive, and unfeminine" for women, especially those at high levels of authority. Such women may be threatening to men used to more obedient and submissive women. One must remember that the negative depiction of Jezebel arose out of a male-dominated society that served the religious and political interests of the author. Since then, social roles and attitudes regarding the genders have changed dramatically. When one reads or hears such descriptions for women of today, one must step back and consider the source.

2 Kings

2 Kings 1:1–8:29

The Ministry of the Prophet Elisha

The Text in Its Ancient Context

Chapter 1 of 2 Kings begins with the detail that after Ahab's death, Moab rebels against Israel, a war that will be taken up in 2 Kings 3. This conflict may have some extrabiblical support in the Mesha Stele (Moabite Stone), which describes Omri's oppression of Moab before Mesha throws off his yoke (Grabbe 2007, 131, 144–46). Omri's dynasty is continued in Ahab's son Azariah (c. 852–851 BCE), who seeks the counsel of "Baal-zebub, the god of Ekron" after a bad fall from his house. The qualifier *zebub* is most likely a distortion of an original *zebul*, or "prince," which alters the god's name to "Lord of the flies." For inquiring of Baal-zebub, Elijah prophesies the king's death (1:1–18).

Wedged between the death of Azariah and the rise of his brother, Ahab's son Jehoram, as king of Israel (2 Kings 3) is the story of the transfer of prophetic power and authority from Elijah to Elisha in 2 Kings 2. It begins with the remarkable statement that God was about to take Elijah up to heaven in a whirlwind, but before this occurs, Elijah and Elisha travel to Gilgal, Bethel, Jericho, and finally to the Jordan River. At the Jordan, Elijah uses his mantle to divide the waters, and the two prophets cross over to the other side on dry ground, reminiscent of other stories where waters are miraculously parted (Joshua 3–4; Exodus 14). Elisha requests a "double share" of Elijah's spirit before he is taken away. According to Deut. 21:17, a double share is the inheritance claim given to the firstborn son of a family. A fiery chariot and horses then appear that separate the two prophets, and Elijah ascends upward in a whirlwind. The use of horses and chariots and whirlwinds may be linked to similar portrayals of ancient Near Eastern storm gods, such as Baal, riding through the clouds, to emphasize YHWH's superior control of the weather (see 1 Kings 18). Elisha declares his kinship with Elijah by crying out, "Father, Father" as the chariot and horses disappear. Elisha then takes up the mantle of Elijah, crosses through the parted waters of the Jordan again, and is joined by the company of prophets. Elisha thus begins his active prophetic ministry during the rule of the Israelite kings Jehoram, Jehu, Jehoahaz, and Jehoash.

Besides his introduction in 1 Kgs. 19:19–21, many of the stories of Elisha preserved in 2 Kings 2–13 have been described as legends and miracle stories, making their historicity suspect. Nevertheless, they provide clues to the social history that formed the context of Elisha's prophetic ministry amid the continued exploitation of the people by the Israelite governing classes (Rentería). For example, scholars think that the company of prophets is primarily composed of the peripheral lower classes and that several of Elisha's miracles are for their benefit (Petersen, 47–48; Schulte, 140). Second Kings 4:1–7 records the miracle of the jar of oil for one of the widows of this company, who, bereft of her husband perhaps because of war, famine, or accidental death in the king's building projects, is compelled to sell her children as debt slaves to pay off creditors. First Kings 18 describes the indifference of the royal court to the starvation of the people during famine. Similarly, the background for the miracle of the stew in 2 Kgs. 4:38–41 consists of the desperate attempts of the company of prophets to find food during famine, during which someone may unknowingly contribute a toxic plant to a shared pot of stew, poisoning the community. This episode is followed by one where Elisha feeds one hundred hungry people with only twenty barley loaves, with some left over (4:42–43). Behind the simple story of the recovery of the ax head from the Jordan (6:1–7) is the reality that the ax head was borrowed (v. 5), probably from one of the elite, who would have been able to possess and lend the expensive commodities necessary for farming like axes, plows, and sickles (cf. 1 Sam. 13:19–21). The average peasant or day laborer from this company would have had to become a debt slave to pay for the ax head.

As we saw in 1 Kings 20 and 22, significant features of monarchic rule are the wars and conflicts of kings. Such wars wreak havoc on the nation's fragile agrarian ecosystem, especially when springs of water are stopped up, fruitful trees are cut down, and the land despoiled (2 Kgs. 3:18, 25). All of these man-made disasters bring much physical and economic suffering to the rest of the population. Narratives of Elisha's prophetic ministry with those in the lower rungs of society, who have been tragically affected by these wars, are interwoven with his dealings with the kings and generals conducting the fighting in this global arena (see chart below). Indeed, the stories of the lowly servant (3:11), the female war captive (5:2–4), and the junior officer (6:12) reveal that the politically subordinate or disenfranchised know more than their masters about the prophetic and healing powers of Elisha (Brueggemann 2001, 52–56; Provan, 185).

The campaign of the three kings against Moab (3:1–27)
The miracle of the widow's oil, the Shunamite's son, the poisoned stew of the company of prophets, the feeding of the people (4:1–44)

The healing of the Aramean general, Naaman, of leprosy (5:1–27)
The recovery of the lost ax head for the company of prophets (6:1–7)

Elisha's adventures with the Arameans and the siege of Samaria (6:8–7:20)
The restoration of the Shunamite's house and land (8:1–6)

Elisha's "anointing" of the kings of Aram and Israel (8:7–9:13)
Adapted from Long and Sneed, 264

The Text in the Interpretive Tradition

Rabbinic tradition is filled with legends of Elijah's appearances on earth after his translation into heaven. He comes to the aid of the innocent victims and especially those who are impoverished. In one story, Elijah sells himself into slavery in order to provide funds for a poor man. He also cures diseases and helps couples with their marital problems. Rabbinic tradition also preserves legends of Elisha. In one of these, the husband of the widow who was compelled to sell her children into debt slavery (2 Kgs. 4:1–7) is the prophet Obadiah, the same official who hid one hundred prophets of YHWH from Jezebel's pogrom (1 Kings 18). Obadiah appears to his widow at his gravesite and directs her to bring a little cruse of oil to Elisha. The miraculous flow of oil not only sustains the widow through her financial difficulties but also the rest of her descendants (Ginzberg 1956, 589–94, 603–4).

Josephus seems to depict Elisha more positively than Elijah in his writings, perhaps because he does not want to be associated with a prophet thought to be the forerunner of the Messiah in his Roman imperial context. He composed a eulogy for the former and not the latter. He omits scenes that portray Elisha negatively, such as the cursing of the boys who called him "baldhead" (2:23–25) and greatly develops others, such as the curing of the waters of Jericho, just prior to the cursing of the boys (2:19–22). He eliminates or rationalizes many of Elisha's miracles, perhaps to counter gentile depictions of Jewish gullibility. Thus, while clearly preserving the popularity of Elijah for his Jewish audience and depicting Elisha as his subordinate, Josephus portrays Elisha's prophetic ministry in a greatly expanded way (Feldman).

Because prophets raised people from the dead (1 Kgs. 17:17–23; 2 Kgs. 4:32–36), cured lepers (2 Kgs. 5:5), multiplied loaves of bread (2 Kgs. 4:42–44; cf. 1 Kgs. 17:8–16), ascended into heaven (2 Kgs. 2:11–12), and worked miracles for rich and poor alike, many thought Jesus was one of the prophets (Matt. 16:13–14; Mark 8:27–28; cf. Luke 4:24–27).

Aspects of Elijah's and Elisha's healings, horses and chariot, the passing of the prophetic mantle, and other elements form a biblical layer for Franz Kafka's short story "The Country Doctor" (Barzel). The African American spiritual "Swing Low, Sweet Chariot" is based on Elijah's ascension into heaven (2 Kgs. 2:11), and also to the angels that carried Lazarus to the bosom of Abraham (Luke 16:22).

The Text in Contemporary Discussion

In 1879, General William Sherman declared "War is hell" to give a reality check to those in the graduating class of Michigan Military Academy who looked on war as all glamour and glory. Much of the background for the so-called miracles that Elisha performs is the hell of war: the death of a family's financial support and the danger of selling one's children into debt slavery (4:1–7); war captives (5:2); famine (4:38–39); starvation (6:24–25; 7:3–4); cannibalism (6:26–31); economic chaos (6:25); and ecological destruction (3:25). To counteract and militate against the trauma of war in its myriad guises, Elisha performs miracles at the local level, but does not critique the roots of war at the systemic level. His prophecy to the kings of Israel, Judah, and Edom deals with whether God will grant them victory over Moab (2 Kings 3), not whether they should engage in war in the first place. These texts encourage us to examine the systemic causes of war to eliminate the monstrous effects of war on the people and the land.

2 Kings 9:1–12:21

The Rise of the House of Jehu and the Demise of the House of Omri

The Text in Its Ancient Context

For Ahab and Jezebel's abuses of power in illegally confiscating Naboth's vineyard in 1 Kings 21, the chickens finally come home to roost in 2 Kings 9–10. The great dynasty inaugurated by Ahab's father Omri is destroyed by Jehu's merciless assassinations of Ahab's son, relatives, and his formidable wife, Jezebel; the Baal cult sanctioned by their regime is purged from the land.

While Ahab's son Joram (c. 851–843 BCE; Jehoram in 3:1) recovers in Jezreel from a battle wound (8:28–29), Elisha sends one of the company of prophets to anoint Jehu (c. 842–814 BCE), a top-ranking military officer, as king over Israel (see 1 Kgs. 19:16). Jehu will "strike down the house of your master Ahab," thus fulfilling Elijah's prophecy against Ahab in 1 Kgs. 21:20–24. Furthermore, Jehu will wreak God's vengeance on Jezebel for the blood of the prophets (see 1 Kgs. 18:4; 19:10), so that "the dogs shall eat Jezebel in the territory of Jezreel, and no one shall bury her" (9:6–10). Jehu's military comrades proclaim him as king, and he embarks on the demolition of Ahab's house (9:13).

Recurring throughout 2 Kings 9 is the ambiguous question *hashalom*, literally, "Is it peace?" but better translated variously depending on the context: "Is everything okay?" "How goes everything?" "Are you well?" "Is all well [at the front]?" "Do you come in peace?" (9:11, 17–19, 22, 31; Olyan). Accompanied by his nephew, Judah's king Ahaziah (c. 843–842 BCE; see 8:25–29), Joram ironically meets Jehu at the former property of Naboth the Jezreelite that was unlawfully seized by Jezebel. He asks Jehu, "Do you come in peace?" but Jehu replies, "What peace can there be, so long as the many whoredoms and sorceries of your mother Jezebel continue?" (9:22), alluding to her support of the worship of Baal. Joram then flees, warning Ahaziah of Jehu's treachery, but Jehu kills Joram and leaves him exposed without an honorable burial on the plot of land that belonged to Naboth. Ahaziah is also killed, but he at least gets an honorable burial in Jerusalem (9:27–28).

Jehu's next murderous stop in Jezreel is Jezebel's palace. If she is going to die, she will die looking like the royal queen she is, painting her eyes and adorning her hair. She is described as a "woman at the window," a conventional trope in ancient Near Eastern carved ivories. She too addresses Jehu sardonically, "Do you come in peace?" or "Is everything okay?" (9:30), and taunts him as a Zimri, who also killed his king but whose rule only lasted seven days (1 Kgs. 16:9–20). Her harem eunuchs, sensing a power change in the wind, obey Jehu's command to throw her down from the window, where her blood splatters the walls and horses trample her. Jehu, whose appetite seemingly is not affected by her gruesome death ("he went in and ate and drank"), begrudgingly orders a burial for "the cursed woman" since she is a "king's daughter." Unfortunately, all that remains of Jezebel's body is her skull, feet, and hands, fulfilling Elijah's prophecy over her. Jehu even adds a coarser adage to the prophecy by noting that her corpse will be like *dung* on the field in Jezreel (9:30–37), most likely an allusion to the corruption of her name from *zebul* ("prince, nobility") to *zebel* ("dung").

Jehu's brutal rampage continues with his slaughter of Ahab's seventy "sons" in Samaria. Just as the eunuchs desert Jezebel, so do the rulers, the elders, and the guardians of the descendants of Ahab in Jezreel deliver the decapitated heads of Ahab's male kin to Jehu. On the road to Samaria, Jehu encounters forty-two relatives of the assassinated Judean king Azariah, who are also members of Ahab's lineage, and has them massacred. Finally arriving in the royal capital Samaria, Jehu eliminates the remaining offspring of Ahab's line (10:1–17). He then "with cunning" exterminates the prophets, priests, and worshipers of Baal and demolishes his temple. Just as Jezebel's corpse will be like "dung in the field," Baal's temple is reduced to "a latrine to this day" (10:18–27).

The Deuteronomistic evaluation of Jehu's rule is equivocal. On the one hand, Jehu is praised for wiping out Baal worship from Israel. God promises that his dynasty in Israel will continue to the fourth generation, and indeed his is the longest and most prosperous one in the northern kingdom. On the other hand, it also points out that Jehu did not follow God's torah with his heart. He did not turn from "the sins of Jeroboam," the two golden calves installed at Dan and Bethel (10:28–31). His rule concludes with a detail that "the Lord began to trim off parts of Israel," in which Jehu loses the area of the Transjordan to the Arameans. Whether or not this territorial loss results from Jehu's disobedience to the law is left for the reader to decide (10:32–33). However, the ninth-century prophecy of Hosea is more explicit: God will "punish the house of Jehu for the blood of Jezreel" (Hosea 1:4).

The southern kingdom still has links with the newly destroyed house of Omri in the person of Athaliah, mother of the slain king Ahaziah, daughter of either Ahab or Omri, and wife of Judah's king Joram (Jehoram) (2 Kgs. 8:18, 25–26). When she hears about Jehu's massacre, she begins her own assassination of the Judean royal family, threatening God's promise of an eternal dynasty for David. However, she is thwarted by her daughter-in-law Jehosheba, who hides Ahaziah's son Joash for six years, while Athaliah rules Judah (2 Kgs. 11:1–30). In the seventh year, the priest Jehoiada, Jehosheba's husband according to 2 Chron. 22:11, stages a coup to return the legitimate king of the Davidic line to the throne. Athaliah hears the noise of the coronation and cries "Treason, treason," but she is put to death outside the temple grounds (11:4–16). Jehoiada enacts a covenantal renewal ceremony "between the LORD and the king and the people," whereupon the people demolish the altars and priest of the cult of Baal, which evidently was instituted during the intermarriage of Judah's kings with the house of Omri. The threatened line of David is now restored in the installation of the seven-year-old Joash after this period of illegitimate female rule (11:17–20).

According to the Dtr's regnal formula, Jehoash (Joash) has a prosperous rule in Jerusalem of forty years, although this may include the six years of Athaliah (836–798 BCE). Under the tutelage of the priest Jehoiada, he is faithful to YHWH, even though he does not eliminate the high places (12:1–3). The narrative about Joash's rule deals with his attempts to repair the temple and arrange for the workers to be financially compensated (12:4–16). However, when the Aramean king Hazael threatens Jerusalem, Jehoash has to deplete the temple and royal treasury that had been built up by his royal predecessors in order to prevent Hazael's attack. The formula concludes with Joash's assassination by his servants (12:12:17–21). According to 2 Chron. 24:23–27, Joash is killed for having murdered the son of Jehoiada, his earlier co-regent (see below). His son Amaziah succeeds him. (For a comprehensive study of 2 Kings 11–12, see Dutcher-Walls 1996.)

The Text in the Interpretive Tradition

According to Ephrem the Syrian, Jezebel paints her eyes and adorns her head (9:30) in order to seduce Jehu and become one of his wives. He links the episode with the story of Adonijah, who requests Abishag the Shunamite as wife, so that he might be elevated to the throne (1 Kgs. 2:17). According to Ephrem, Jehu would want Jezebel as wife to pacify his troubled and agitated new rule. Ephrem also contrasts Jezebel's ignominious death with that of her husband, Ahab. While Jezebel is trampled by horses and eaten by dogs (2 Kgs. 9:33–37), Ahab receives an honorable burial (1 Kgs. 22:37), because he repents from his sins (1 Kgs. 21:27–29) and she does not (Conti, 185–86).

According to Jewish tradition, the prophet Jonah is a disciple of Elisha, who commissions him to anoint Jehu as king. Athaliah's reign of terror is God's punishment of the Davidic dynasty for the extermination of the priests of Nob (1 Samuel 22). Just as Abiathar is the only son of Ahimelech to survive this slaughter, so is Joash the only son of Ahaziah to survive Athaliah's pogrom. After Jehoiada's death, Joash sets up an idol in the temple, but Jehoiada's son and high priest, Zechariah, bars his entry to the temple on the Day of Atonement, which also happens to be the Sabbath. Joash has Zechariah killed, and his death remains unavenged until Nebuzaradan, captain of Nebuchadnezzar's army, destroys Jerusalem. Before his servants kill him, Joash falls into the hands of the Syrians, who "abused him in their barbarous, immoral way" (Ginzberg 1956, 609–10).

The advent of feminist criticism in the late twentieth century focuses critical attention on the queens, Jezebel and Athaliah, whose portrayals as wives and mothers in these texts belie their formidable power and authority in their husbands' kingdoms (Solvang; Bowen; C. Smith 1998).

The Text in Contemporary Discussion

These texts describe a regime change through violent assassinations. Our own contemporary world is no stranger to such violence, as seen in the political assassinations of Abraham Lincoln, John F. Kennedy, and Martin Luther King. Each period after such murders is marked by much social instability. The killings by Jehu are depicted as particularly motivated by religious zeal: "to wipe out Baal from Israel" (2 Kgs. 10:28). These texts highlight the acute dangers that arise from intense religious passions, namely, the intolerance of other religions, leading to their persecution and extermination in God's name. History already provides many cautionary tales of this religious intolerance: the

Crusades and the extermination of indigenous religions by Spanish colonizers in South America and Native American religions by white settlers. We can also include the terrorist attacks by Islamic fundamentalists today. Is violence at the root of the monotheistic faiths? Does religious fervor have to lead to violence? Where are the voices that resist and critique this violence and move beyond mere tolerance, to learn about and respect other religions in their comprehension of the sacred?

2 Kings 13:1–17:41

Events Leading to the Fall of Israel

The Text in Its Ancient Context

According to 2 Kgs. 10:30, YHWH declares that Jehu's dynasty in Israel will last to the fourth generation. Second Kings 13 focuses on the second and third generation of the house: Jehoahaz (c. 817–800 BCE, 13:1–9) and Jehoash/Joash (c. 800–784 BCE, 13:10–19). Both are condemned for following in "the sins of Jeroboam son of Nebat." Both regimes are plagued by military confrontations with Aram/Syria. The prophet Elisha appears for the last time during Joash's rule. Hearing news of Elisha's imminent death, Joash goes to him, weeping and crying out, just as Elisha did at Elijah's departure: "My father, my father! The chariots of Israel and its horsemen!" (13:15; cf. 2 Kgs. 2:12). Elisha commands Joash to perform a sign act with a bow and arrow to symbolize "the arrow of victory over Aram" at the battle of Aphek (13:17). However, because Joash only strikes the ground with the arrows three times, instead of five (13:18–19), his victory over the Arameans will be incomplete, keeping Syria as an ongoing player in the politics of Israel and Judah (see the Syro-Ephraimite War below). Even in death, Elisha's miraculous powers live on, raising a dead man to life when his corpse touches the bones in Elisha's grave (13:2–21).

The narrative regarding Jehoash/Joash continues in 2 Kings 14, highlighting the rule of the Judean king Amaziah (c. 798–769 BCE). As soon as he gains power, Amaziah executes the two men who assassinated his father Joash (12:20–21), but spares their children according to law of Deut. 24:16 (2 Kgs. 14:5–6). He then engages in a successful campaign against his southeastern neighbor Edom (14:7). However, he foolishly challenges Jehoash of Israel, who responds with a parable of the thorn bush and the cedar, warning Amaziah that any military encounter will be disastrous (on Jehoash's fable, see Solomon 1985). Amaziah engages in battle with Jehoash anyway, but Jehoash not only defeats and captures him but also strips the Jerusalem temple and royal palace of its treasuries (14:8–14). Amaziah is killed after he flees to his stronghold in Lachish (14:17–20) and is succeeded by his son Azariah/Uzziah (14:21–22).

During the fifteenth year of Amaziah's rule in Judah, Jeroboam son of Joash (Jeroboam II, c. 788–747 BCE) rules in Samaria, representing the fourth generation of the Jehu dynasty (14:23–28). Although he follows in the sins of his namesake, Jeroboam son of Nebat (Jeroboam I), his rule is a prosperous one of forty-one years in Israel. Fulfilling the word of the prophet Jonah, Jeroboam expands Israel's borders from Lebo-Hamath (upper Syria) to the Sea of Arabah (the ideal boundaries of Solomon's kingdom, 1 Kgs. 4:21; 8:65). The reign of his Judean counterpart, Azariah/Uzziah, is also a long one of fifty-two years (c. 792–740 BCE, 15:1–7). Dtr only gives him a qualified approval, because he does not remove the high places. Second Chronicles 26, however, greatly expands on Uzziah's rule and provides a reason for God afflicting him with leprosy, which is missing in 2 Kgs. 15:5. The Deuteronomic focus on the religious aspects of their monarchic rule obscures the fact that Israel and Judah under Jeroboam II and Azariah/Uzziah witnessed dramatic political and economic growth (Premnath, 43–98).

Representing the fifth generation of Jehu's dynasty, Jeroboam II's son Zechariah (c. 747 BCE) is not covered under God's prophecy of 2 Kgs. 10:30. His rule therefore only lasts six months and he is assassinated by Shallum (c. 747 BCE, 15:8–12), beginning a series of unstable regimes that will eventually climax in Israel's destruction. After only one month of rule, Shallum is killed by Menahem (c. 747–737 BCE, 15:13–22), a violent king credited with ripping open the pregnant women of a city that refused to surrender to him (15:16; cf. Cogan).

During this time, the powerful Assyrian king Tiglath Pileser III (Pul in the Bible, c. 745–727 BCE) begins his westward expansion to gain access to the economic and military possibilities provided by the Mediterranean Sea. Levying a steep tax on the wealthy, Menahem offers "a thousand talents of silver" to forestall King Pul from attacking Israel, tribute that is confirmed in Assyrian accounts (Grabbe 2007, 134). Menahem is able to hold on to power for ten years when his son Pekahiah (c. 737–735 BCE) succeeds him at his death. Pekahiah rules only two years, when he is assassinated by one of his officers, Pekah (15:23–26; regarding the problematic dating of Pekah's rule, see Na'aman, 74–82). During Pekah's rule, Tiglath Pileser captures the Israelite territories of Gilead, Galilee, and all the land of Naphtali, and activates the initial deportations of Israel to Assyria (15:27–29; Younger, 206–8). Pekah himself will eventually be killed by Hoshea (15:30–31), but his narrative will continue in the account of the Syro-Ephraimite War in 2 Kings 16.

During Pekah's rule in Israel, Jotham (c. 759–743 BCE, 15:32–38) begins his administration in Judah when his father Azaraiah/Uzziah is stricken with leprosy (15:5). He is given a generally positive assessment by Dtr, which is expanded in 2 Chronicles 27. Dtr's judgment on his son, Ahaz, however, is quite negative for a Judean king, describing him as walking "in the way of the kings of Israel" in his idolatrous practices (16:1–4). Scholars have dated his rule variously: 727–715 BCE; 735–715 BCE; 743–735 BCE. Attempting to coerce Judah into joining their alliance against Tiglath Pileser III's expansionism, Kings Rezin of Aram/Syria and Pekah of Israel attack Judah in what is known as the Syro-Ephraimite War (16:5). In response, Ahaz petitions Tiglath Pileser himself to "rescue" him from his northern neighbors, becoming his vassal and sending him tribute. Tiglath Pileser responds by destroying Syria's capital city Damascus and exiling its upper classes (15:7–9). Dtr greatly expands on Ahaz's covenantal infidelity by describing his commissioning and instillation of a new altar in the temple that represented his loyalty to Assyria (Sweeney 2007, 384–86). Ahaz will be succeeded by his son Hezekiah (16:10–20).

Having undergone a complex editorial process (Long, 180–83), 2 Kings 17 is a significant one in the DH, because it provides an extended theological rationale for the fall of Israel. It begins by describing its last days under king Hoshea (c. 732–722 BCE), who had rebelled against Tiglath Pileser's successor, Shalmaneser V of Assyria, and was subsequently imprisoned by him. After a three-year siege, Shalmaneser's successor, Sargon, conquers Samaria in 722/721 BCE and exiles its upper classes (17:1–6).

Dtr's theological commentary highlights the covenantal infidelity of Israel, who forsakes the God who brought them from slavery in Egypt to worship other gods (17:7–12). They refuse to listen to the prophets sent by God (17:13–15), and persist in the sin of Jeroboam son of Nebat (17:21–22). God therefore removes them "out of his sight," and Israel is exiled from their own land to Assyria "to this very day" (17:23). A later redactional addition will testify that Judah will suffer the same fate (17:19–20).

The chapter then narrates the consequences of the Assyrian policy of bringing in foreign populations to replace the exiles in Samaria (Oded). Because the Assyrians do not worship YHWH, God sends lions among them (17:24–25). The king of Assyria tries to deal with this problem by commanding one of the exiled priests be brought back to teach the foreigners "the law of the god of the land" (17:25–27). However, this priest originally hales from Bethel, one of the illegitimate sanctuaries established by Jeroboam I, implying that his teachings replicate the "sin of Jeroboam" among the people (17:28). Dtr then details the religious syncretism of the "people of Samaria," who will later be called Samaritans. They are ultimately judged as worshiping YHWH, but also as serving "their carved images" (17:29–41).

The Text in the Interpretive Tradition

For the rabbis, Ahaz was an extremely wicked man (*Lev. Rab.* 30.3) who, among other things, seized schools and synagogues (11.7), and introduced the worship of Moloch. However, because he was the son

(*Gen. Rab.* 63.1) and father (*Eccl. Rab.* 7; 15.1) of devout kings (*Sanh.* 104a), his place was secured in the world to come. In Milton's *Paradise Lost*, Ahaz is a devotee of one of the fallen angels "against the house of God," Rimmon the Syrian deity associated with Damascus (*PL* 1.467–75) (Baker 1992a, 27).

The early church father Ephrem the Syrian had a number of things to say about the final days of Elisha. Regarding his prophecy to Joash, "the Lord's arrow of victory" (13:17) for him "signifies our Lord and Savior hanging from the wood and giving up his spirit." When Elisha dies, the prophet Hosea takes his place as the head of the company of prophets, because the beginning of Hosea's oracles places him during the time of Jeroboam, son of Joash. The resurrection of the man who was tossed into Elisha's grave foretells the future resurrection of all those who have died (Conti, 197–99). Some church fathers used these stories to further their antisemitic views. Origen argues that in light of Jewish purity laws, especially the prohibition of touching dead beings, the miracle of resurrection of the man who touches Elisha's bones reveals "how unsuitable the Jewish interpretation is." John Chrysostom uses the example of Ahaz's sacrificing his son (16:3) and other examples of illegitimate cult to explain the cruelty of the Jews in condemning Christ (Conti, 200, 207).

Josephus's portrayal of the last six kings of Israel expands on their biblical depictions, making them more violent and more reckless in their dealings with Assyria (Begg).

The Text in Contemporary Discussion

In these chapters, Dtr provides us with a sustained rationale for why Israel was destroyed and its people exiled. It culminates in 2 Kings 17, which argues that throughout its history the northern kingdom abandoned YHWH to worship other gods. We must keep two things in mind when interpreting these chapters. First, Dtr is assessing the history of these kings *after the fact* from his exilic/postexilic social location. Israel was already destroyed, and Judah is not far behind.

His explanation is filtered through experiences of hindsight. Second, the intent of his history is *theological*. There are many other reasons—military, economic, political, social—why Israel was destroyed, the most obvious being Assyria's brutal, overwhelming resolve to gain entry to the Mediterranean Sea. Nevertheless, for Dtr, Israel's destruction is an act of divine judgment because it failed to keep God's covenant.

Dangers in interpretation arise when one assesses history from the perspective of "the rear-view mirror." It is first and foremost *an* interpretation of events, not *the* interpretation of events. Moreover, *theological* rationales of calamitous events pose serious issues, particularly when the judgment is on a group other than one's own. For example, some German clergy asserted that the extermination of the Jews by the Nazis was God's punishment of the Jews (Sweeney 2008, 1–22). The destruction caused by recent natural events like tsunamis and hurricanes has been explained by religious fundamentalists as God's castigation for abortion, homosexuality, and feminism. Theological explanations are difficult to substantiate and often originate from the harmful gender, racial, or other ideologies regarding marginal groups. As such, they should be avoided.

2 Kings 18:1–20:21

The Reign of Hezekiah

The Text in Its Ancient Context

Along with David and Josiah, Hezekiah (c. 727/715–698/687 BCE) is one of the most highly acclaimed kings of Judah according to Dtr. Historians have tried to reconcile 2 Kings 18–20 with Assyrian sources about Sennacherib's invasion in 701 BCE, many regarding 2 Kgs. 18:13–16 as the only historically reliable part of the narrative: Sennacherib attacked and captured the fortified cities of Judah; Hezekiah submitted to him; Sennacherib demanded a huge tribute of silver and gold; and Hezekiah gave it to him. The rest of 2 Kings 18–20 has undergone a long traditioning process around this relatively historical piece (Grabbe 2007, 195–200;Grabbe 2003).

The Dtr introduction first describes Hezekiah's cultic reform to centralize worship in Jerusalem, anticipating Josiah's later one (18:1–4). Unlike many of the other Judean kings, Hezekiah removes the high places, pillars, and the sacred pole, a symbol of YHWH's wife Asherah (Dever), and a revered Mosaic relic, the bronze Nehustan (Num. 21:1–9). The recurrence of the word "trust/rely" defines Hezekiah's reliance on God (18:5, 19–22, 24, 30; 19:10), transforming his story into a theological discourse on faith in YHWH (Brueggemann 2000, 493). This faith and confidence will be tested by the Assyrian envoys. Unlike his father, Ahaz, Hezekiah rebels against Assyria (18:7). However, the juxtaposition of Hezekiah's rule in Judah with the downfall of Hoshea and Israel (18:9–12) implies that Judah will not suffer the same fate, because Hezekiah holds fast to God, who was with him when he rebelled (18:6–7).

Nevertheless, the most historically reliable part of the story seems to challenge Dtr's commendation: Sennacherib's invasion in response to this rebellion, and Hezekiah's handover of tribute for Sennacherib's withdrawal (18:13–16). Instead of withdrawing, Sennacherib sends three officials, the Tartan, the Rabsaris, and the Rabshakeh (chief commander, chief eunuch, and chief cupbearer) to negotiate the surrender of Jerusalem. Details of this Assyrian encounter with Judean officials (Eliakim, Shebnah, and Joah) have parallels in Isaiah 36–37. The Rabshakeh skillfully articulates the shortcomings in Hezekiah's sources of trust. Relying on his ally Egypt is foolhardy, because Egypt is a "broken reed of a staff that will pierce the hand of anyone who leans on it" (18:21). Trusting in God's very self has been abrogated by Hezekiah's destruction of God's high places and altars in his centralization of worship (18:22). Even if Assyria gives Judah two thousand horses, Hezekiah has no riders to put on them, especially if he relies on Egyptian assistance (18:23–24). Finally, God's very self sends Assyria to destroy Judah (18:25). Each of these four arguments has a certain ring of credibility (Nelson, 238).

The Judean officials request the Rabshakeh to speak in the diplomatic language of Aramaic, not Hebrew, so that the populace will not hear his demoralizing words. However, the Rabshakeh arrogantly continues in Hebrew to address those doomed "to eat their own dung and drink their own urine" in a prolonged Assyrian siege (18:26–28). He tells them not to be deceived by Hezekiah into relying on God's deliverance. The gods of Hamath, Arpad, Sephaarvaim, Hena, and Ivvah were unable to save their citizens from Assyrian conquest. YHWH will likewise be unable to deliver Jerusalem (18:29–35). Upon hearing the officials' report on the Rabshakeh's words, Hezekiah sends them to consult the prophet Isaiah, who tells Hezekiah, "Do not be afraid," and that God will put a "spirit" in Sennacherib, so that he will hear a "rumor and return to his own land," where he will be killed (19:1–7).

In the next episode, Sennacherib does hear a report that the Egyptian pharaoh Tirhakah of Cush/Ethiopia has set out against him, but instead of returning to his own land, sends his messengers to intimidate Hezekiah again (19:8–13). Hezekiah then appeals to YHWH in the temple (19:14–19), and Isaiah delivers three oracles to him. The first is directed against Sennacherib, highlighting God's own divine power vis-à-vis the king's human arrogance and future humiliation (19:20–28). The second is a "sign" to Hezekiah that the agricultural fields devastated by Sennacherib's armies will recover in three years, and that a remnant will repopulate the land (19:29–31). The third prophesies that Sennacherib will not enter Jerusalem, because God will defend it for God's own and David's sakes (19:32–34). The chapter concludes with the "angel of the Lord" striking down 185,000 in the Assyrian camp and Sennacherib's returning to Assyria, where he is eventually killed by his sons while he is worshiping in the temple of his god Nisroch (19: 35–37). Hezekiah's trust in YHWH is thus vindicated.

The final two episodes about Hezekiah in 2 Kings 20 seem to describe events before Sennacherib's siege of Jerusalem, because Isaiah prophesies that God will add fifteen years to Hezekiah's life and deliver Jerusalem from the king of Assyria (20:6) and the royal treasury is still full (20:13; cf. 18:15–16). The first episode describes Hezekiah's life-threatening boil (20:7), Isaiah's command that he put his life in order before his death, and Hezekiah's fervent prayer to God to remember his faithfulness and devotion (20:1–3). God responds through Isaiah that God will heal Hezekiah, add years to his life, and deliver Jerusalem from the Assyrians. Isaiah then orders Hezekiah to take a lump of figs and apply it to the boil, to heal it (20:4–7).

The second episode involves envoys of King Merodach-baladan, a Babylonian king who heard Hezekiah was ill. Hezekiah welcomes them and shows them all the wealth in his house, armory, and storehouses (20:12–13). Hezekiah may have entered into an anti-Assyrian alliance with the Babylonian king, which would explain why Sennacherib was not able to capture Jerusalem in a lengthy siege. He would not have been able to divide his forces to deal with conflict on the western side of his empire, and with Merodach-baladan on his eastern flank (Sweeney 2007, 413). However, upon hearing of Hezekiah's overt display of his wealth to these foreigners, Isaiah prophesies that in the future Babylon will come and seize everything in his house, and exile some of his sons, who will become eunuchs—those who cannot bear royal sons—in the palace of the king of Babylon (2:14–18). Although Hezekiah verbally acknowledges the prophecy as good, his inward thought, "Why not, if there be peace and security in my days" (20: 19), reveals a negative side to this positively portrayed character: his disregard for disastrous events in Judah and his dynasty after his own peaceful and secure reign.

The Text in the Interpretive Tradition

Rabbinic legends describe Hezekiah as banishing the ignorance of the law that had occurred under his father Ahaz, to the point of ordering that anyone who does not occupy himself with the torah is subject to the death penalty. Needless to say, eventually one could search from Dan to Beer-sheba and not find a single person ignorant of torah. The illness that afflicted Hezekiah was punishment for "peeling off" the gold from the temple to send to Sennacherib (2 Kgs. 18:16). Therefore, the disease that plagued Hezekiah caused his skin to "peel off." Hezekiah is praised for having the traditions of Isaiah, Ecclesiastes, Song of Songs, and Proverbs put in writing.

Rabbinic legends narratively expand on characters that are not developed in 2 Kings. Sennacherib's vast army is described in great detail. He himself was contemptuous when he first saw Jerusalem, wondering why he bothered to gather armies and conquer other lands to gain it. It was smaller and weaker than the other cities he had subdued. Two of the officials sent to meet the Assyrian negotiators, Shebnah and Joah (cf. 2 Kgs. 18:18), were actually opponents of Hezekiah's rebellion. They shot a dart into the Assyrian camp containing a letter, saying: "We and the whole people of Israel wish to conclude peace with thee, but Hezekiah and Isaiah will not permit it." When Shebnah and his supporters left Jerusalem to join the Assyrians, the angel Gabriel manipulated Sennacherib into thinking that Shebnah was fooling him. Sennacherib then ordered Shebnah tied to a horse and dragged to death (for more on Hezekiah, see Ginzberg 1998, 266–77).

Hezekiah is chiefly remembered in Christian tradition for his piety and for the extraordinary answer to his prayer for a stay of death (e.g., Cyril, *Lectures* 2.15; 12.22). In New England Puritanism, he was sometimes described as a type of Christ (e.g., Thomas Frink, *A King Reigning in Righteousness* [1758]) and as a moral example for temporal magistrates (Baker 1992b, 352). The poem "Destruction of Sennacherib," by Lord Byron, in his *Hebrew Melodies* (1815), depicts the Assyrian king's perspective on the siege.

The Text in Contemporary Discussion

We are presented in 2 Kings 18–20 with an idealized king, a paradigm of piety with an abiding trust in YHWH. God was with Hezekiah wherever he went, prospering in his domestic and foreign policies: his centralization of worship and his rebellion against Assyria. He becomes the total opposite of his father, Ahaz, before him and his son Manasseh after him. Nevertheless, we will soon see that the alternation between good king/bad king is a deliberate Dtr construction. Historical and archaeological reconstructions of the period reveal that Hezekiah's cultic centralization and rebellion against Assyria were foolhardy and had disastrous consequences for the economic and social landscape of Judah. Moreover, we will soon see that the supposedly "evil" king Manasseh actually helped Judah recover from his father's disastrous foreign and domestic policies.

Dtr creates a history "after the fact," from the social location of a community that has experienced the trauma of exile and needs an explanation. The explanation Dtr provides is a theological one: the people were unfaithful to God's covenant. We must keep this in mind as we try to relate Hezekiah's story to our own times. Placing one's trust in God in decisions regarding foreign or domestic policies must work in tandem with dedicated analysis of the broader social and political issues surrounding these policies.

2 Kings 21:1–23:30

The Reigns of Manasseh and Josiah

The Text in Its Ancient Context

Dtr sets before us two stereotypical models of kingship in these chapters: one utterly "bad" (Manasseh), the other categorically "good" (Josiah). Neither really resembles his historical personage. Dtr describes "evil" Manasseh as reversing all the cult reforms that his father Hezekiah had instigated, comparing him to the absolute worst king of the northern kingdom, Ahab (21:3, 9). His religious abominations even exceeded those of the pagan nations that YHWH drove out of the land (12:9, 11). Because of Manasseh's colossal failures to keep Deuteronomic law (Deut. 12:29–31; 18:9–12; 19:8–10), an unknown prophet declares that YHWH will "wipe Jerusalem as one wipes a dish," casting the remnant off, giving them over to the hands of their enemies (2 Kgs. 21:12–16).

Although blamed for the eventual fall of Judah, Manasseh's lengthy rule (698/687–642 BCE) was historically much more beneficial to the nation than Dtr presents. Following the conventions of ancient Near Eastern historiography, Dtr alternates bad and good kings before and after Manasseh: Ahaz (bad); Hezekiah (good); Manasseh and Amon (bad); Josiah (good) (Evans, 497). Because Josiah is the "golden boy" of the Deuteronomists, Manasseh is set up as his foil. Although he is presented as one of the "good" kings, Hezekiah's rebellion against Assyria was politically and economically disastrous. Sennacherib ravaged the countryside, and Hezekiah lost valuable land in the Shephelah (Finkelstein and Silberman, 251–64). Inheriting a weakened and humiliated nation, Manasseh was left with the task of rebuilding the state after this catastrophe.

Archaeology reveals that Judah experienced a remarkable resurgence under Manasseh's long reign (Grabbe 2007, 201). Collaborating with networks of village clan-based leaders, whose authority was diminished under Hezekiah, Manasseh began to restore those areas of the countryside that were ravaged by Sennacherib. Providing these networks with economic autonomy, his renewal of the rural areas permitted the veneration of the popular agrarian gods, Baal and Asherah, which would later provoke the wrath of the Deuteronomists (Finkelstein and Silberman, 264–67; Halpern 1991, 60–65). Working his position as vassal to his advantage, Manasseh's connections with Assyrian markets enriched his treasuries, trading in luxury goods from Arabia and exporting olives from the Judean highlands for the mass production of oil in the Assyrian-ruled city of Ekron (Finkelstein and Silberman, 267–70; Gitin, 84–87). Despite the biblical condemnation of his regime, Manasseh's rule was a peaceful and prosperous one for Judah. He is succeeded by his son Amon, who is assassinated by court servants, and Amon's son Josiah is placed on the throne by "the people of the land" (21:19–26).

Josiah's birth and rule were already foretold in 1 Kings, when Jeroboam I was offering incense at Bethel, one of his illegitimate sanctuaries. A man of God prophesies against the altar, "A son shall be born to the house of David, Josiah by name; and he shall sacrifice on you the priests of the high places who offer incense on you, and human bones shall be burned on you" (1 Kgs. 13:2). Dtr exalts Josiah among the other Judean kings by describing him as "walking in *all* the way of his father David," and, like Moses and Joshua, "he did not turn aside to the right or to the left" (2 Kgs. 1:2; Deut. 5:32; Josh. 1:7). There was no king before or after him "who turned to the LORD with all his heart, with all his soul, and with all his might, according to the law of Moses" (23:25).

During repairs on the temple, the high priest Hilkiah finds "the book of the law." Hilkiah reports its "discovery" to Josiah, who hears the words of this book as a prophetic judgment from God, "because our ancestors did not obey the words of this book" (22:3–13). Like Moses and Joshua (Exodus 24; Joshua 24), Josiah renews the covenant with the people (23:2–3) and sets about purging the land of idolatrous worship. He begins first with Jerusalem and its environs (23:4–14) and then proceeds to Bethel, the site of the prophecy in 1 Kgs. 13:2, which foretells the destruction of the altar that Jeroboam I erected. Josiah not only tears down the altar but also defiles it by having human bones burned on it, fulfilling the earlier prophecy before moving on to other cultic sites in Samaria (23:15–20). Josiah then centralizes his liturgical reform by instituting the national celebration of Passover held in Jerusalem (22:21–23).

Scholars believed that the "book of the law" was an earlier form of the book of Deuteronomy. However, because of its similarities to early seventh-century Assyrian vassal treaties, they now think that Deuteronomy was composed in the seventh century, just before or during Josiah's reign. Deuteronomy is thus not an ancient scroll that is suddenly "discovered" in the temple but the composition of a Deuteronomistic school (Römer, 45–65). In spite of Josiah's good deeds, he is not able to reverse God's judgment against Judah and Jerusalem because of Manasseh's offenses (23:26–27). Josiah is killed by Neco, pharaoh of Egypt, at Megiddo, and his son Jehoahaz is anointed king by the people of the land (23:28–30).

The Text in the Interpretive Tradition

Second Chronicles 33:11–13 has Manasseh captured by the Assyrians, who imprison him in Babylon. He repents of his sins, and God returns him to Jerusalem, where he eliminates the foreign gods and restores the worship of YHWH in the land. The remorse of the one who was considered to be the cause of Jerusalem's destruction provided hope and encouragement to the postexilic returnees to Yehud. The apocryphal work Prayer of Manasseh claims to be the one he utters in 2 Chron. 33:13, although this is unlikely. (See "Prayer of Manasseh" in this commentary.)

Manasseh's contrition is expanded by Josephus (*Ant.* 10.40–46), who concludes that Manasseh "underwent such a change of heart in these respects and lived the rest of his life in such a way as to be counted a blessed and enviable man after the time when he began to show piety toward God" (*Ant.* 10.45). Rabbinic legends describe the king of Babylon casting Manasseh into a heated oven, whereupon Manasseh remembers a prayer his father Hezekiah had taught him about calling on YHWH during times of tribulation. However, angels stop his prayer from reaching God, but God, knowing that he would be shutting the doors to anyone who repents if he did not accept Manasseh's penance, receives Manasseh's prayer through a small opening under the throne of his glory. A wind carries Manasseh back to Jerusalem (Ginzberg 1998, 279–80; Hulbert).

According to rabbinic legends, Josiah sought prophetic confirmation after hearing God's judgment against Jerusalem. He consulted Huldah, not Jeremiah, because he believed that a woman would be more compassionate than a man and deliver a more temperate oracle (*b. Meg.* 14b). Knowing that the temple would be destroyed, he hid the ark of the covenant and all its accessories to protect them from enemy desecration (*Yoma* 52b). Although he instituted a purge of foreign worship, Josiah was deceived by the people, who hid their idolatrous ways from his inspectors (*Lam. Rab.* 1.53). Because of this deception and for disobeying the counsel of Jeremiah to allow the Egyptians passage through his land, Josiah was struck by three hundred darts in the clash between him and the Egyptians (Ginzberg 1998, 282–83). Josephus remarks that Jeremiah composed a lament for Josiah's funeral (*Ant.* 10.78).

The Text in Contemporary Discussion

The biblical portrayals of Manasseh and Josiah are ancient examples of demonization and angelization. Demonization is a rhetorical strategy of depicting rival individuals or groups as embodying all that is considered evil or wicked in a particular context. Angelization is its very opposite, representing an individual or group as all good or virtuous. Neither characterization adequately exemplifies the person or groups in question. Demonization is often used to cast targeted individuals or groups as the other. We have seen that Dtr attributes the destruction of Jerusalem to Manasseh by demonizing his rule, even though he historically helped Judah recover from the disastrous foreign policies of his father Hezekiah, who is angelized by Dtr in spite of them.

We often demonize or angelize individuals in our own time. The Bush Administration demonized Saddam Hussein in order to invade Iraq in the 1990s. The Nazis demonized a whole ethnic group, the Jews, in order to justify the Holocaust. Pro-choice advocates are often contemptuously regarded as "baby-killers." The poor are often vilified as "parasites" and "on the dole." Liberals often label conservatives as "rigid," "ignorant," and "intolerant." Many Roman Catholics "angelized" their parish priests, until the sex scandals that have rocked the church revealed an insidious side to their behavior. Evangelicals have angelized many televangelists until revelations of their financial or sexual corruption have surfaced.

Demonization or angelization of persons or groups close off discussion and further inquiry that would reveal a more unbiased, truthful state of affairs. Our examination of Manasseh and Josiah cautions us to recognize demonization or its opposite when they occur in our own time, and to examine such stereotypical characterizations more fully.

2 Kings 23:31–25:30

The Final Days of Judah and Its Kings

The Text in Its Ancient Context

Although in the larger context of Egyptian and Babylonian imperial politics it was probably inevitable that Judah would be conquered and destroyed by the Babylonians, Dtr still judges its demise theologically. The final kings of Judah—Jehoahaz, Jehoiakim, Jehoiachin, and

Zedekiah—all "did what was evil in the sight of the LORD as their ancestors had done" (23:32, 37; 24:9, 19). Therefore, God's very self sends their enemies—Chaldeans, Arameans, Moabites, and Ammonites—to attack Judah to fulfill the words of the prophets, because God refuses to forgive Judah for the "sins of Manasseh" (24:2–4). God's wrath is unequivocal for Dtr: "Jerusalem and Judah so angered the LORD that he expelled them from his presence" (24:20).

Jehoahaz (609 BCE) rules Jerusalem three months before he is imprisoned at Riblah by Pharaoh Neco, the same king who had his father Josiah killed (23:29–33). After levying a large tribute tax on Judah, Neco installs Josiah's son and Jehoahaz's half-brother Eliakim as a puppet king in Jerusalem, and changes his name to Jehoiakim (608–597 BCE). In 605 BCE, the Babylonian king Nebuchadnezzar defeats the Egyptians at the battle of Carchemish in Syria and Judah becomes a vassal of Babylonia. Jehoiakim submits to Babylonian rule for three years, but he seizes his chance to rebel, probably after Babylon's costly battle with the Egyptians in 601 BCE. Recovering two years later, Nebuchadnezzar strikes back against Judah with the aid of Judah's neighbors Aram, Moab, and Ammon. Jehoiakim conveniently dies during Nebuchadnezzar's siege of Jerusalem in 597 BCE, and his unfortunate eighteen-year-old son Jehoiachin succeeds him (24:8–9).

Jehoiachin surrenders to Nebuchadnezzar, who carries him off to Babylon along with the queen mother, his harem, the officials, the elite of the land, and anyone in positions to instigate a rebellion (24:10–16). Nebuchadnezzar appoints Jehoiachin's uncle Mattaniah as his puppet king and changes his name to Zedekiah. Nebuchadnezzar's conquest, deportation, and installation of "a king of his liking" in 597 BCE are confirmed in the Babylonian Chronicle (*ANET* 563–64).

Twenty-one-year-old Zedekiah becomes Judah's final king (597–586 BCE). His rule is hampered by several factors, the first being the brain drain of Judah's top officials in the 597 deportation, leaving second-tier advisors. Second, he is appointed by the colonizer, while the "legitimate" king, Jehoiachin, is in exile. Third, his administration is plagued by the pro-Egyptian and pro-Babylonian partisan politics at court. These politics are particularly evident in the book of Jeremiah (see Jeremiah 27–28; 37–38). Unfortunately, Zedekiah sides with the pro-Egyptian party and rebels against Nebuchadnezzar, who besieges Jerusalem in 587 and ultimately conquers it in 586 BCE. Zedekiah is captured when he tries to escape, and is brought to Nebuchadnezzar at Riblah. Zedekiah witnesses the death of his sons before he himself is blinded and taken in chains to Babylon (24:20b–25:7). The temple is burned, and all the treasures that were not seized in 597 are taken away. Furthermore, the remaining elites are exiled in a second deportation (25:9–17) (on the two forced migrations, see Ahn). The only ones allowed to remain are "some of the poorest people of the land," who probably constituted the crucial agrarian economic base of Judah (25:12; cf. 24:14).

To establish some stability in the land, the Babylonians appoint a prominent Judean, Gedeliah, as governor at the new capital, Mizpah. However, Ishmael and his men, most likely anti-Babylonian partisans, assassinate Gedeliah and flee to Egypt to escape Babylon's wrath (25:22–26). Their story is recounted in greater detail in Jeremiah 40–43.

The book of 2 Kings ends ambiguously, with the release of King Jehoiachin from prison by King Evil-merodach of Babylon. He is given a privileged seat at the foreign king's table and a pension for as long as he lives (25:27–30). Although the Davidic dynasty has been disgracefully terminated in Judah, the fact that its exiled king is freed from prison and attains some sort of status, albeit in a foreign court, can be interpreted as a sign of hope for a renewed kingship.

The Text in the Interpretive Tradition

Leviticus Rabbah 19.6 describes the "abominations" of Jehoiakim in 2 Chron. 36:8 variously. He disobeys the prohibitions of Lev. 19:19 and Deut. 9:11 by wearing garments that mix wool and linen together. He is guilty of disguising his circumcision; tattooing the names of idols on his body; having incestuous relations with his mother, daughter-in-law, and father's wife; and executing men to violate their wives and seize their wealth. When Nebuchadnezzar comes up against Jerusalem, he tells the Sanhedrin, who meets him at Daphne of Antioch, that he only wants the insurgent Jehoiakim. If the Sanhedrin deliver him up, Nebuchadnezzar will withdraw. Like the city of Abel Beth-maacah, which saved itself by surrendering Sheba son of Bichri (2 Sam. 20:14–22), the Sanhedrin seize Jehoiakim and slide him down the city walls of Jerusalem into the hands of the Babylonians. Nebuchadnezzar takes him in chains around the cities of Judah, kills him, and puts his carcass on an ass. Another version states that Jehoiakim is cut into olive-sized pieces and thrown to the dogs.

Jehoiachin fares better than his father in *Leviticus Rabbah* 19.6. When Nebuchadnezzar tells the Babylonians that he has installed Jehoiachin as Jehoiakim's replacement, he is told a proverb: "Do not rear a gentle cub of a vicious dog, much less a vicious cub of a vicious dog." Regretting his decision, he then informs the Sanhedrin at Daphne of Antioch that if they deliver Jehoiachin to him, he will withdraw from attacking the temple. When Jehoiachin hears this, he takes the keys of the temple to the roof and bids God to take them, at which point a hand from heaven seizes them. Another version says that the keys remain suspended in midair. Nebuchadnezzar then puts Jehoiachin into solitary confinement. The Sanhedrin begins to worry that the house of David will cease, if Jehoiachin does not beget a son. They devise a plan involving Nebuchadnezzar's wife, Shemirah, to persuade her husband to let Jehoiachin have sexual relations with his wife. When they are about to have sex, the wife notices the onset of her menstrual period. Because Jehoiachin obeys the law and refrains from sex during her impurity, God pardons all his sins.

The Text in Contemporary Discussion

The book of Kings thus ends the sordid history of Israel's failure to keep God's torah. It is not history as we understand it today, describing "what really happened." Rather, it is a selective history, told from a biased perspective. The Deuteronomistic History records that from the moment the Israelites crossed the Jordan and settled in the land

(Joshua and Judges), they were seduced away from their covenanted partner, YHWH, to worship the gods of the land. They even wanted kings "like the other nations," rejecting YHWH as king (1–2 Samuel). First and Second Kings continue the story with wise king Solomon, blinded by his love for foreign women and their gods, the division of the kingdom into Israel and Judah, the "sin of Jeroboam," which ultimately led to Israel's fall, and then to that of Judah, who refused to learn from Israel's mistakes. For Dtr, the end of this glorious nation is the people's continual infidelity to their God and God's covenant.

The conclusion to the book of Kings prompts us to think about the way we also construct history. All histories are written from a selective partisan perspective, even those that claim to be objective. One commonly hears the saying "History is written by the victors," and this is true. The book of Kings compels us to wonder about the voices that are not recorded in its stories: those of the poor, the marginalized, the soldiers who lost their lives or those who were maimed in the continual wars of the kings, the citizens who starved during the horrible sieges, and the peasants whose crops were crushed or seized by invading armies.

What about histories in our own time? Do American history books adequately tell the stories of the indigenous peoples whose lands were appropriated in the name of Manifest Destiny; or the horrors of slavery and the Civil War, the most shameful period of our history? Does this history focus primarily on European immigrants, ignoring those from Asia, Africa, South America, and the Caribbean? What we learn from the book of Kings is that its history is not disinterested, is not nonpartisan. How can we critically examine the histories of peoples, groups, and nations in our own time?

WORKS CITED

Ahn, John J. 2011. *Exile as Forced Migrations: A Sociological, Literary, and Theological Approach on the Displacement and Resettlement of the Southern Kingdom of Judah*. BZAW 417. Berlin: de Gruyter.

Baker, David W. 1992a. "Ahaz." In *A Dictionary of Biblical Tradition in English Literature*, edited by David L. Jeffrey, 27. Grand Rapids: Eerdmans.

Baker, David W. 1992b. "Hezekiah." In *A Dictionary of Biblical Tradition in English Literature*, edited by David L. Jeffrey, 352–53. Grand Rapids: Eerdmans.

Bartel, Roland. 1975. "Melville's use of the Bible in *Billy Budd*." In *Biblical Images in Literature*, edited by Roland Bartel, James S. Ackerman, and Thayer S. Warshaw, 30–64. Nashville: Abingdon.

Barzel, Hillel. 1975. "The Biblical Layer in Franz Kafka's Short Story 'A Country Doctor.' " In *Biblical Images in Literature*, edited by Roland Bartel, James S. Ackerman, and Thayer S. Warshaw, 89–102. Nashville: Abingdon.

Baumgarten, Murray. 1992. "Abishag." In *A Dictionary of Biblical Tradition in English Literature*, edited by David L. Jeffrey, 6–8. Grand Rapids: Eerdmans.

Beach, Eleanor F. 2005. *The Jezebel Letters: Religion and Politics in Ninth-Century Israel*. Minneapolis: Fortress Press.

Begg, Christopher T. 1996. "The Last Six Kings of Israel According to Josephus: Ant 9,228–278." *ETL* 72:371–84.

Berlin, Adele. 1982. "Characterization in Biblical Narrative: David's Wives." *JSOT* 23:69–85.

Bird, Phyllis A. 1997. *The Harlot as Heroine: Narrative Art and Social Presupposition in Three Old Testament Texts*. Minneapolis: Fortress Press.

Bowen, Nancy R. 2001. "The Quest for the Historical Gebirâ." *CBQ* 63:597–618.

Branch, Robin G. 2009. *Jeroboam's Wife: The Enduring Contributions of the Old Testament's Least-Known Women*. Peabody, MA: Hendrickson.

Brueggemann, Walter. 2000. *1 and 2 Kings*. Smyth &Helwys Bible Commentary. Macon, GA: Smyth & Helwys.

Brueggemann, Walter. 2001. *Testimony to Otherwise: The Witness of Elijah and Elisha*. St. Louis: Chalice.

Cogan, Mordechai. 1983. "'Ripping Open Pregnant Women' in Light of an Assyrian Analogue." *JAOS* 103:755–57.

Conti, Marco, ed. 2008. *1–2 Kings, 1–2 Chronicles, Ezra, Nehemiah, Esther*. Ancient Christian Commentary on Scripture, Old Testament 5. Downers Grove, IL: InterVarsity Press.

Curzon, David. 1994. *Modern Poems on the Bible: An Anthology*. Philadelphia: Jewish Publication Society.

Dever, William G. 2005. *Did God Have a Wife? Archaeology and Folk Religion in Ancient Israel*. Grand Rapids: Eerdmans.

Dutcher-Walls, Patricia. 1996. *Narrative Art, Political Rhetoric: The Case of Athaliah and Joash*. Sheffield: Sheffield Academic.

Dutcher-Walls, Patricia. 2004. *Jezebel: Portraits of a Queen*. Interfaces. Collegeville, MN: Liturgical Press.

Evans, Carl D. 1992. "Manasseh, King of Judah." *ABD* 4:496–99.

Feldman, Louis H. 1994. "Josephus' Portrait of Elisha." *NovT* 36:1–28.

Finkelstein, Israel, and Neil A. Silberman. 2001. *The Bible Unearthed: Archaeology's New Vision of Ancient Israel and the Origin of Its Sacred Texts*. New York: Free Press.

Gaines, Janet H. 1999. *Music in the Old Bones: Jezebel through the Ages*. Carbondale: Southern Illinois University Press.

Garsiel, Moshe. 1993. "The Story of David and Bathsheba: A Different Approach." *CBQ* 55:244–62.

Garsiel, Moshe. 2002. "Revealing and Concealing as a Narrative Strategy in Solomon's Judgment (1 Kings 3:16–28)." *CBQ* 64:229–47.

Ginzberg, Louis. 1956. *Legends of the Bible*. Philadelphia: Jewish Publication Society of America.

Ginzberg, Louis. 1998. *The Legends of the Jews*. Vol. 4, *From Joshua to Esther*. Baltimore: Johns Hopkins University Press.

Gitin, Seymour. 1997. "The Neo-Assyrian Empire and Its Western Periphery: The Levant, with a Focus on Philistine Ekron." In *Assyria 1995: Proceedings of the 10th Anniversary Symposium of the Neo-Assyrian Text Corpus Project, Helsinki, September 7–11, 1995*, edited by S. Parpola and M. R. Whiting, 77–103. Helsinki: The Neo-Assyrian Text Corpus Project.

Grabbe, Lester L., ed. 2003. *"Like a Bird in a Cage": The Invasion of Sennacherib in 701 BCE*. JSOTSup 363. London: Sheffield Academic.

Grabbe, Lester L. 2007. *Ancient Israel: What Do We Know and How Do We Know It?* New York: T&T Clark.

Halpern, Baruch. 1991. "Jerusalem and the Lineages in the Seventh Century BCE: Kinship and the Rise of Individual Moral Liability." In *Law and Ideology in Monarchic Israel*, edited by Baruch Halpern and Deborah W. Hobson, 11–107. JSOTSup 124. Sheffield: JSOT Press.

Halpern, Baruch. 2001. *David's Secret Demons: Messiah, Murderer, Traitor, King.* Grand Rapids: Eerdmans.

Hulbert, W. G. 2008. "Good King and Bad King: Traditions about Manasseh in the Bible and Late Second Temple Judaism." *Stone-Campbell Journal* 11:71–81.

Ipsen, Avaren E. 2008. "Solomon and the Two Prostitutes." In *Marxist Feminist Criticism of the Bible*, edited by Roland Boer and Jorunn Okland, 134–50. Sheffield: Sheffield Phoenix.

Ishida, Tomoo. 1999. "Solomon's Succession to the Throne of David." In *History and Historical Writing in Ancient Israel: Studies in Biblical Historiography*, 102–36.Leiden: Brill.

Jobling, David. 1991. "Forced Labor: Solomon's Golden Age and the Question of Literary Representation." *Semeia* 54:57–76.

Knoppers, Gary N. 1995. "Aaron's Calf and Jeroboam's Calves." In *Fortunate the Eyes That See: Essays in Honor of David Noel Freedman in Celebration of His Seventieth Birthday*, edited by Astrid B. Beck, Andrew H. Bartelt, Paul R. Raabe, and Chris A. Franke, 92–104. Grand Rapids: Eerdmans.

Lang, Bernhard. 1983. *Monotheism and the Prophetic Minority: An Essay in Biblical History and Sociology.* Sheffield: Almond.

Lasine, Stuart. 1989. "The Riddle of Solomon's Judgment and the Riddle of Human Nature in the Hebrew Bible." *JSOT* 45:61–86.

Lassner, Jacob. 1993. *Demonizing the Queen of Sheba: Boundaries of Gender and Culture in Postbiblical Judaism and Medieval Islam.* Chicago: University of Chicago Press.

Long, Burke O. 1991. *2 Kings.* FOTL. Grand Rapids: Eerdmans.

Long, Jesse C., Jr., and Mark Sneed. 2004. " 'Yahweh Has Given These Three Kings into the Hand of Moab': A Socio-Literary Reading of 2 Kings 3." In *Inspired Speech: Prophecy in the Ancient Near East. Essays in Honour of Herbert B. Huffmon*, edited by John Kaltner and Louis Stulman, 253–75. London: T&T Clark.

Moore, Megan B., and Brad E. Kelle. 2011. *Biblical History and Israel's Past: The Changing Study of the Bible and History.* Grand Rapids: Eerdmans.

Na'aman, Nadav. 1986. "Historical and Chronological Notes on the Kingdoms of Israel and Judah in the 8th Century BC." *VT* 36:71–92.

Nelson, Richard D. 1987. *First and Second Kings*. IBC. Atlanta: John Knox.

Oded, Bustenay. 1979. *Mass Deportations and Deportees in the Neo-Assyrian Empire*. Wiesbaden: Reichert.

Olyan, Saul. 1984. "*Hašalôm*: Some Literary Considerations of 2 Kings 9." *CBQ* 46:652–68.

Petersen, David L. 1981. *The Roles of Israel's Prophets*. Sheffield: JSOT Press.

Premnath, D. N. 2003. *Eighth Century Prophets: A Social Analysis*. St. Louis: Chalice.

Provan, Iain W. 1995. *1 and 2 Kings*. Peabody, MA: Hendrickson.

Pyper, Hugh S. 1993. "Judging the Wisdom of Solomon: The Two-Way Effect of Intertextuality." *JSOT* 59:37–53.

Rentería, Tamis H. 1992. "The Elijah/Elisha Stories: A Socio-Cultural Analysis of Prophets and People in Ninth-Century BCE Israel." In *Elijah and Elisha in Socioliterary Perspective*,edited by Robert B. Coote, 75–126. Atlanta: Scholars Press.

Römer, Thomas C. 2007. *The So-Called Deuteronomistic History: A Sociological, Historical, and Literary Introduction*. New York: T&T Clark.

Schulte, Hannelis. 1994. "The End of the Omride Dynasty: Social-Ethical Observations on the Subject of Power and Violence." *Semeia* 66:133–48.

Seow, Choon-Leong. 1999. "The First and Second Books of Kings: Introduction, Commentary, and Reflections." In *The New Interpreter's Bible*. Vol. 3, *1 and 2 Kings, 1 and 2 Chronicles, Ezra, Nehemiah, Esther, Tobit, Judith*, edited by Leander E. Keck, 1–295. Nashville: Abingdon.

Smith, Carol. 1998. "'Queenship' in Israel? The Cases of Bathsheba, Jezebel and Athalia." In *King and Messiah in Israel and the Ancient Near East: Proceedings of the Oxford Old Testament Seminar*, edited by John Day, 142–62. Sheffield: Sheffield Academic.

Smith, Mark S. 2002. *The Early History of God: Yahweh and the Other Deities in Ancient Israel*. Grand Rapids: Eerdmans.

Smith, Morton. 1971. *Palestinian Parties and Politics That Shaped the Old Testament*. New York: Columbia University Press.

Snyder, Josey B. 2012. "Jezebel and Her Interpreters." In *Women's Bible Commentary*, edited by Carol A. Newsom, Sharon H. Ringe, and Jacqueline E. Lapsley, 180–83. Louisville: Westminster John Knox.

Solomon, Ann M. V. 1985. "Jehoash's Fable of the Thistle and the Cedar." In *Saga, Legend, Tale, Novella, Fable: Narrative Forms in Old Testament Literature*, edited by George W. Coats, 126–32. JSOTSup 35. Sheffield: JSOT Press.

Solvang, Elna. 2003. *A Woman's Place Is in the House*. JSOTSup 349. New York: Continuum.

Stahlberg, Lesleigh C. 2009. "From Biblical Blanket to Post-Biblical Blank Slate: The Lives and Times of Abishag the Shunamite." In *From the Margins 1: Women of the Hebrew Bible and Their Afterlives*, edited by Peter S. Hawkins and Lesleigh C. Stahlberg, 122–40. Sheffield: Sheffield Phoenix.

Sweeney, Marvin A. 2007. *1 and 2 Kings: A Commentary*. OTL. Louisville: Westminster John Knox.

Sweeney, Marvin A. 2008. *Reading the Hebrew Bible after the Shoah: Engaging Holocaust Theology*. Minneapolis: Fortress Press.

Wolde, Ellen van. 1995. "Who Guides Whom? Embeddedness and Perspective in Biblical Hebrew and in 1 Kings 3:16–28." *JBL* 114:623–42.

Yee, Gale A. 1992. "Jezebel." *ABD* 3:848–49.

Younger, K. L., Jr. 1998. "The Deportations of the Israelites." *JBL* 117:201–27.